THE

GOSPEL NARRATIVES:

THEIR

ORIGIN, PECULIARITIES, AND TRANSMISSION.

By HENRY A. MILES.

NINTH THOUSAND.

BOSTON:
AMERICAN UNITARIAN ASSOCIATION,
21 BROMFIELD STREET.
1858.

CAMBRIDGE:
STEREOTYPED AND PRINTED BY
METCALF AND COMPANY,
PRINTERS TO THE UNIVERSITY.

PREFACE.

WHAT was the origin of our four Gospel Narratives? If the authors of these wrote independently, how can we account for their verbal coincidences? If they copied from one another, how can we account for their discrepancies? Under what circumstances did each writer perform his work? How far did his situation and character and purpose give shape to his composition? How have these Gospels been transmitted down to our times? — Such are the chief questions which it is the object of this book to answer. It is believed that instruction on these points should form a part of a Christian education. They constitute a branch of the evidences of Christianity on which all historical belief must rest, but to which, for the most part, no general attention is paid. How many of the flippant objections of infidelity would lose all their power to unsettle faith, if some knowledge on this subject were widely diffused! Perhaps it has been neglected through the want of a small book, that may briefly and clearly present the information now found only in professional, and, to most readers, inaccessible treatises. This want it is here proposed to supply. While the author has had reference to the higher classes in our Sunday schools, for whose use he hopes this work may serve as a manual, he has also had his eye upon other readers, and has sought to make a book suitable for family and parish libraries. He has studied accuracy in drawing his materials from the most approved sources, and has been ambitious of earning for himself only the negative merits of lucid arrangement and perspicuous statement.

CONTENTS.

THE GOSPEL NARRATIVES.

CHAPTER I.

STATEMENT OF THE QUESTION.

THE word *Gospel*, meaning good news, properly denotes the revelations which the history of Christ contains. These revelations are the "*glad tidings* which shall be to all people." But in process of time that word has been applied to the history itself, and denotes a book describing the birth, life, words, sufferings, and death of the Son of God.

We have four distinct books of this kind, written evidently by four different men. We believe them to have been written by Matthew, Mark, Luke, and John, not long after the ascension of Christ. Matthew and John were his personal followers; Mark received his materials from Peter, another follower of Christ; while Luke, as he tells us in his preface, set in order the things which had been delivered to him by those who from the beginning had been eyewitnesses and ministers of the word. Thus they did not undertake to write without being well informed of the events which they have related. Hence the confidence with which they appealed to the sources of their knowledge: — "That which was from the beginning, which we have heard, which we have seen with our eyes, declare we unto you."

Did they all four write together? Did any of them copy what another had written? Did they all write independently, each with no knowledge of the others' compositions? Here are several theories suggested; which of them do the facts of history compel us to take?

As regards the Gospel of John, we cannot be at much loss to decide. When he composed his narrative, he had undoubtedly seen what Matthew, Mark, and Luke had previously written. This is evident from the whole character of his work. Thus he for the most part records only what Jesus said and did in Judea, as the other Evangelists confined themselves chiefly to what Jesus said and did in Galilee. What they fully related he omits, their omissions he supplies, and some slight errors of theirs he corrects. He alludes to our Saviour's baptism, and to the last Supper, though he has not described those events, evidently supposing that they would be well known by means of the other Gospels; and in the end of his history he says, —"Many other signs truly did Jesus, which are not written in this book." He knew many of them were written in the books of the other Evangelists. His tacit appeal to their writings must be understood as an approval of what they had previously published.

But now what shall we say of the other three Gospels? When we compare them with one another, we find two facts, which at first we hardly know how to reconcile with any theory as to their origin. We find that in some places they agree with one another, not merely in describing the same thing, but in describing it word for word alike; while in other places they not only use different words in describing the same thing, but give quite different accounts.

Examples need not be adduced of what must be so familiar to every one who has compared the Gospels of Matthew, Mark, and Luke together. Open them where we will, we occasionally find, in descriptions of the same occurrence, whole verses which in all three of the writers are word for word alike, and which seem as if they must have been copied one from the other. But we do not read far before we find that there are also great differences between them, not merely in arrangement and quotation, but in the statement of facts. These differences seldom relate to very material facts. Merely to show their character, one or two examples may be adduced.

There was a dispute among the disciples on the question, who of them should be greatest in the kingdom of heaven. Jesus rebuked their folly by setting a little child before them, and saying, "Except ye be converted and become as little children, ye shall not enter into the kingdom of heaven." Now Matthew says that the disciples referred this dispute to Jesus. "At the same time came the disciples unto Jesus, saying, Who is the greatest in the kingdom of heaven?" — Matt. xviii. 1.

But an exactly opposite account is given in Mark, who says that Christ inquired for the subject of their dispute, and that the disciples declined to name it. "And being in the house, he asked them, What was it that ye disputed among yourselves by the way? But they held their peace; for by the way they had disputed among themselves who should be the greatest." — Mark ix. 33, 34.

How clearly marked is the difference between these two statements! Yet we do not find it difficult to reconcile them. We know that Peter, James, and John, the sons of Zebedee, claimed to be greatest among the disciples, and on their way to Capernaum they probably advanced their claims, which led to the dispute. Other disciples, without claiming the first rank, might think it unjust to be treated as inferiors; and Matthew, who was a humble publican, was probably of this party. He doubtless brought the matter in dispute before Christ. The Saviour reserved the discussion until they had entered the house, and then made the inquiry recorded by Mark. Peter, James, and John made no answer, for they would expect reproof. Both statements are thus reconciled by supposing that Matthew related the part to which he was knowing, and that Mark, who derived his materials from Peter, related the part to which he was knowing, but that neither related the whole. There is no real contradiction between them. But there is a seeming contradiction. Taken simply by themselves, it would appear, that, if Matthew's account were true, Mark's must be false. If it was not for what we incidentally learn, in some other part of the Gospel, of the ambitious claim of Peter, James, and John, it would not be easy to make any consistent agreement between them.

We may take another case. The account of Peter's denying his Lord is recorded by all four Evangelists. Both Matthew and Mark give us to understand that the second denial was made to one of the waiting *maids* in the high-priest's palace. Matthew xxvii. 71. Mark xiv. 69. But Luke's account is, that the second denial was made to a *man*. Luke xxii. 58. This is one of the places which John's Gospel corrects and explains. He tells us that the second denial was made to a *great number* of servants and officers, who were standing with Peter by the fire in the high-priest's palace. John xviii. 25. This makes the other accounts appear true. But had it not been for this explanation, we should not know which statement to believe.

Now the question that arises is this: How shall we explain the many verbal coincidences, and, at the same time, the many marked discrepances, which are found in the first three Gospel histories? Shall we say that their authors wrote in concert, or that one saw the work of his predecessor and copied it? This will explain the resemblances. But how shall we then account for the differences? Shall we then take the other view, and conclude that they are perfectly independent historians, writing without the slightest knowledge of each other's works? This will account for the differences. But what shall we then say of their resemblances?

CHAPTER II.

THE EVANGELISTS NOT COPYISTS.

We should considerably relieve the difficulty before us, if we could prove that the first three Evangelists did not copy one from the other. And this is the impression which must be left strongly on the mind when we compare their narratives together. They arrange events in different order. They assign different occasions to the same discourse or parable. We should not have looked for this, either if they had written together, or if one had copied from the other. It is not easy to believe that one writer copied the other merely that he might make some small additions of original matter, for such additions in any one Gospel are too inconsiderable to render such a supposition credible. Then there is no trace of any other Gospel in that one, whichever it be, that you assume to be a copy. Verbal coincidences nowhere lie together in masses. Identity in the use of words nowhere extends unbroken through long passages. The same word or phrase occurs only here and there, in separated and scattered places.

Moreover, the Evangelists had no motive to copy from one another. As preachers of Christianity, they were all well acquainted with the transactions which it was their purpose to record. Each one, therefore, was competent to draw up his own independent account. Besides, each one's account appears to be his own, — his own style, his own associations, his own arrangement. It is of still more importance to observe, that each one's knowledge of every event appears to be his own independent knowledge. To a description of almost all the prominent events of our Saviour's life, each Evangelist has contributed something. One noticed one circumstance, another a second, another a third, so that, as in the case already adduced of the denial of Peter, we have not a full description until we put all their works together. When we come to examine each Gospel by itself, we shall see still further evidence to show that these histories were written independently, at different times, in different places, and for different purposes. The discrepancies between them are just such as we might expect from three independent historians.

No contemporaneous and independent histories are precisely alike. Inspiration would not secure the Evangelists from discrepancies common to all other writers, because inspiration does not mean omniscience. Even if we found inexplicable contradictions between the Gospels, it would by no means follow that the history they give is false. The only just inference would be, that their authors were not infallible. Between different histories of England, for example, there are most mysterious contradictions as to striking and prominent events. But no one concludes that these histories are all fabulous, and that these events never transpired. So, also, in the examination of witnesses, and in the common rumors of our neighbourhood and town, we never suffer the fact of many contradictory accounts of any alleged event to preclude all belief. We involuntarily have a stronger faith that something has happened. We question only the perfect accuracy of narrators. This is all we could reasonably doubt, did we find inexplicable contradictions in the Gospels. But such contradictions are not here found to perplex the fair inquirer. He finds only such discrepancies in the relation of minor events as must always mark independent accounts. When one individual paints a city from the east side, and another one from the west, both must, indeed, represent the highest and most prominent steeples and buildings; but in other respects the two sketches may and must be very different from each other. And yet each may give a faithful representation.

CHAPTER III.

THEIR LIFE IN JERUSALEM.

Before we can see the cause of the verbal coincidences in the Gospels, we must give attention to some historical facts.

After our Lord's resurrection, he showed himself to his disciples, on various occasions, for the space of forty days. Just before his ascension, he directed them to come together at Jerusalem, after he should leave them, and there for a while to tarry. Luke xxiv. 49. Acts i. 4. There was deep wisdom in this direction. Jerusalem was in the near neighbourhood of the wonderful scenes of the crucifixion, the resurrection, and the ascension, and the Saviour would have his disciples bear witness to these facts on the very spot of their occurrence. It was the most public witness they could bear, before all the inhabitants of that city, and before all the people from all parts of Judea, who came up at the great national festivals. It was right that the disciples should challenge the most open and public investigation. Nothing had been done in a corner, and every thing which had been told to them in private, they were to proclaim upon the house-top. Their constant and bold preaching in such a place as Jerusalem would be a proof that they were not ashamed of their religion, although its founder had been crucified as a vile criminal. It would be an expression of their belief, that their great cause did not die with their leader, while a more central place for the propagation of the truth could not be selected. Here were Parthians and Medes, Cretes and Arabians, strangers from Egypt and Rome. Converts made among these would spread the religion all over the world. So important was it that the disciples should keep together at Jerusalem, as commanded by their Master.

And they did keep together there. We are told in the Acts of the Apostles, i. 12, that from the scene of their Saviour's ascension they returned at once unto Jerusalem, and went up into an upper room, where they abode together. While they dwelt here, all the events transpired which are recorded in the first seven chapters of the Acts,—the election of an Apostle to take the place of Judas, the gift of tongues on the day of Pentecost, the cure of the lame man at the gate of the temple, the imprisonment and release of John, the deaths of Ananias and Sapphira, and the martyrdom of Stephen. We do not know exactly how long a space of time these events covered. It could not have been less than several years. During these, the disciples were continually repeating in each other's hearing the story of Christ's life and words.

Now let us try to enter into their situation. Their Head and Master, to whom they had looked for counsel, and on whom they had leaned for support, had been taken from them. They were left like a little band of brothers who have suddenly lost their father. They were in the heart of a great city, in which they felt alone, for among its busy throngs they at first found but little sympathy, being either pitied as deluded men or despised as deceivers. If we had not been told that they *dwelt* together, how naturally should we have presumed this, and that they continually conferred with one another, and endeavoured to comfort, sustain, and animate each other's hearts! And in these frequent interviews, what would so much occupy their thoughts, and be the constant topic of their conversation, as the wonderful events of their Master's life, and the impressive instructions that he gave them? Doubtless, at their first interview their remembrances of these were very much alike in their minds. The more accurately they could recall the very words that Christ used, the more coincident would these remembrances be. Nor would it be difficult for them to recall his precise words. In those days the art of writing was not common in the class to which the Apostles belonged. The memory on this account received a greater cultivation. Much longer histories than either of our Gospels were very often treasured up in the memory alone. To tasks of memory, it is not unlikely the disciples themselves had been accustomed, when

Jews. The Rabbis required their pupils to repeat what was taught them, and in this way an immense mass of traditionary accounts was handed down from one generation to an other.

Then what strong motives had the Apostles to make them remember both the words of their absent Teacher, and the wonderful events of his life! All their interests and hopes were bound up in these things. Gratitude and reverence, their loneliness and danger, their duty to their Master's cause, and the uncertainty that hung over their prospects, — every thing would send their minds back to that one fountain of light and hope, the life and words of Christ. The sick healed, the lame, the blind, the deaf, the insane, restored, the very dead raised, and those touching parables they had heard, of the good Samaritan, the prodigal son, the rich man and Lazarus, — how was it possible that they could forget these? Their recollections of them must have been their spring of action by day, and their meditation by night. This was their Comforter. The spirit of truth was with them, and brought all things to their remembrance.

Now there was one cause constantly at work to make them *express* their remembrances alike. They were constantly teaching in one another's hearing. Few and feeble as they were, they soon had converts. A large number was added to them on the day of Pentecost. Soon the fame of their wonderful works spread abroad. The sick were brought in beds, and laid in the streets where the Apostles lived. Believers were added to the Church daily. We can easily conceive what an intense curiosity all these would feel to learn the precise words and actions of Jesus. It was now the business of the Apostles to gratify this curiosity. Their discourses must have consisted, in great part, of simple narratives concerning the life of Jesus. It was a matter of necessity that they should be continually speaking about him, describing his miracles to establish his authority, the minor events of his life to illustrate his character, and his parables and discourses to set forth his doctrine. Thus month after month, and year after year, they were repeating the same narrative which we find recorded in the Gospels. As they did this continually, in each other's hearing, to different persons who wished to hear precisely the same things, how obvious is it that they would soon acquire a similar style of narration. At each repetition, the narrative would assume more and more a common form in each of their minds. We can name three peculiarities which their method of telling the story of Christ would naturally acquire.

1. There would be the greatest verbal coincidence in their repetitions of the words of Jesus. Because, if they remembered his words correctly, the accounts of them must be identically the same. Naturally attaching a peculiar sacredness to the precise words which he used, they would take the greatest care to recall them correctly, and for this purpose they would help and correct one another's remembrances.

2. There would be less verbal coincidence in the narrative parts of their story, those, namely, in which they described events without repeating the words of Jesus. Here each disciple would adopt a method somewhat peculiar to himself, though naturally there would be some verbal resemblance in the use of particular phrases and connecting sentences.

3. In the matter of order and arrangement there would be the least resemblance of all. They would probably select their topics with reference to the previous knowledge or particular curiosity of their hearers. Each one, therefore, would group particular parables, miracles, and discourses of

our Lord together in his own way. Where nothing was to be gained by chronology, there would be no regard and no pretence to it, and thus would be formed a diversity of associations in regard to time and the sequence of events.

Here, then, the Apostles lived together, and told the same story, over and over again, to the converts who were added daily to the Church. Matthew and John were here, for their names are given in the list found in Acts i. 13. Luke was undoubtedly here, for he was an early convert, and in his preface to his Gospel he tells us that he obtained his knowledge from those who from the beginning were eyewitnesses and ministers of the word, that is to say, from the Apostles. And Mark was here, for his mother's house was one of the places where the Apostles used to meet. Acts xii. 12.

CHAPTER IV.

THEIR WRITTEN NARRATIVES SHAPED BY THEIR PREVIOUS ORAL ONES.

At length the day came when they could no longer live together in Jerusalem. Their bold preaching, and their convincing miracles, made so many converts as to attract the attention of the priests and rulers. Then followed days of persecution, when they were all driven from the city, and were scattered abroad. But persecution always strengthens what it would suppress. The effect of banishing thousands of converts from Jerusalem was to give increased life and power to the new religion. Its friends were now sent into all the principal cities and villages round about, who became so many preachers, made more ardent by persecution. They found that the fame of their banishment had everywhere gone before them, and people were everywhere asking what the new doctrine was. Hence bodies of believers were soon gathered in Samaria, at Damascus, Antioch, Cesarea, Cyprus, Corinth, and the wrath of man was made to praise God.

In these places, the first desire of all converts was to hear those who had been personal followers of the Saviour. Hence the Apostles were pressed to tell what they knew, and to testify to what they had seen. But soon it appeared that the call came from more places than they could visit, and from more converts than they could personally address. To supply the want of their attendance in person, several of them wrote out what they had so often preached, and copies of their narrations were sent to instruct and comfort believers. Thus Matthew, about the year 65, wrote out a short record of the Saviour's life and words, for the use of the churches in Judea. At that time Mark was with Peter in Rome, and there he put his short Gospel history into writing. Luke, before either of these accounts were written, as is probable, sent his history to his Gentile friend Theophilus; and John, long after the others had published their narratives, contributed the additions and corrections which are found in his Gospel, for the benefit of the church at Ephesus.

Thus each writer had his own independent object to accomplish, and wrote in his own independent manner. Still, each one gave his account in *writing* very much in the same way they had so long been accustomed to give it in *preaching*, when they lived together in Jerusalem. And to men so little practised in writing as the Apostles were, and intent only upon telling the simple truth in the shortest and most direct manner, could any thing be more natural than the course they took? May we not feel increased confidence in the truth and honesty of these men, when we see that in banishment, amid persecution, and no longer sustained by each other's sympathy and support, they persisted in publishing the same narrative they had formerly preached in Jerusalem? Nor should we fail to admire the good providence of God, which, out of the persecution which separated the disciples from their home and from one another, and sent them forth to a perilous life to be soon terminated by a martyr's death, created a necessity of making at once, when all was well remembered and well known, a clear record of words and events so intensely interesting to our dearest wants and hopes.

But those single-minded writers little knew to what a work they had seated themselves. They only thought of enlightening their personal friends, or at most, of comforting a few feeble churches, scattered through Judea. They little thought that the roll, which seemed to them so brief, fragmentary, and perishable, would float over the whole world, and down to all time. The thing which, had it ever been thought of, must have seemed impossible with man, has been possible with God.

CHAPTER V.

APPLICATION OF THIS VIEW TO THE FACTS OF THE NARRATIVE.

THE question with which we are next concerned is this, — Will the view above given account for all the facts in the case? Will it explain both the resemblances and the discrepancies found in the Gospels? If this explanation be the true one, it will shed not only a consistent, but a clear, convincing, and interesting light upon the Evangelical narrative. We will proceed, then, to apply it to the facts in the case.

We have seen that the Apostles, in giving their accounts of Jesus, would be anxious first of all to repeat his words exactly; and that between their statements of what he said, if their statements are worthy of reliance, there must be very great resemblances. We have seen, also, that in the mere narrative parts of their histories each writer would be free to use his own words, and that here the resemblances would be less. Now how stands the fact?

We will take first the Gospel of Matthew. Of the whole book, only one sixth part consists of passages verbally coincident with one or both of the other two Gospels. Of this small part, seven eighths occur in the recital of the words of others, mostly the words of Jesus, while only about one eighth is found in mere narration.

We next look to the Gospel of Mark. The proportion of coincident passages to the whole contents of the Gospel is about one sixth. Of this not one fifth occurs in the narrative.

Luke has still less agreement of expression with the other Evangelists. The passages in which it is found amount only to about a tenth of his Gospel, and not one twentieth part of this in the narrative.

But then we should not expect the aggregate of verbal resemblances to be as great in the narrative part of the Gospels as it is in that where the words of others are professedly quoted, because the narrative part is not one half of the whole Gospels. The narrative part occupies but one fourth of Matthew's Gospel, one half of Mark's Gospel, and one third of Luke's. "It may be easily computed, therefore, that the proportion of verbal coincidence found in the narrative part of each Gospel, compared with what exists in the other part, is about in the following ratios: in Matthew as one to somewhat more than two, in Mark as one to four, and in Luke as one to ten."

These definite proportions were obtained by the careful investigations of Andrews Norton of Cambridge, to whose learned work on the Genuineness of the Gospels the reader is referred, Vol. I., Appendix, p. ci. How important they are to support the view before presented, that our present *written* Gospels grew out of previous *spoken* ones, must be obvious at once. If the Evangelists had copied from one another's writings, we should have looked for just as many coincidences in the narrative part of their Gospels as in the other part. If, on the other hand, they were not familiar with each other's mode of narration, we should not have expected in the narrative part any coincidences at all.

We may add another consideration. In the narrative parts of the Gospels, the coincidences are of a *kind* which we should expect to find. Those who learn, from each other's frequent repetition, the form of narrating any events, seldom repeat long portions word for word alike. They coincide only in the general mould of thought, and in the use of peculiar phrases and connecting sentences. We have before taken notice of the fact, that in the Gospels verbal coincidences nowhere lie together in masses. They occur, a few words here, and a few words there, in peculiar phrases and colloquial expressions. "*And Jesus answered them and said*," "*And after this it came to pass*," "*Verily, verily, I say unto you*";—these and like expressions give an appearance of similarity between the narrative portions of different Gospels; and it is just such sentences as these which, when we often hear and tell the same story, we are most prone to catch and repeat from one another's lips.

And, lastly, that our first three Gospels took their form and character from the narratives which the Apostles used to give, when they lived and taught together in Jerusalem, is rendered still further probable by the little regard which their writers pay to chronological arrangement. It was before remarked, that in their oral teachings they would be likely to neglect the order of time, and to group together particular parables, or discourses, or miracles, with reference to the state of information or curiosity of their hearers. Now, in our written Gospels we find this disregard to the natural sequence of events, and this grouping of different things together. There is frequently a particular class of miracles, or a particular series of instructions, evidently cast by each writer in the same general style of description; but each is made up without the slightest mark of any regard to the order of time. They bear traces of having been distinct narratives by themselves. They are connected together by associations peculiar to each Evangelist. Hence, to make out a satisfactory Gospel chronology is one of the most difficult things in Biblical study. What we lose in this respect, we more than gain in the greater assurances we have of the perfect artlessness and careless simplicity of an honest pur pose, in which the histories of Christ were written.

Indeed, how much do we owe to the fact, that these histories were written in this way and by these men! The very circumstance that they were unlearned men made them better qualified to be scribes of the truth. They have given us nothing but *facts*, — not a word of comment, or inference, or even note of admiration. A learned man of their times would have been pretty sure to thrust in something of his own into his pages; and how suspicious, how out of keeping with the simple and sublime words of Jesus, would it have appeared! Who does not see that the charm and power of the Gospel narrative would have been lost, if it had been handed over to the verbose periods and oratorical descriptions of such a writer as Josephus? The Evangelists have given us nothing but *facts*. When we read their words, we feel that we are in the presence of facts, whose solemn reality moved their deepest natures, and overawed all merely personal feelings. And it is this air of simple, sincere, straightforward, and solemn reality, everywhere spread over their writings, that gives them their power. The Christian feels them to be true. The skeptic himself feels them to be true. The French infidel, Diderot, was one day caught learning his little daughter to read the Gospels. When reminded of his inconsistency, he replied, "After all, there is no history like this." And there is not. The learning of the schools, and the wisdom of ages, have not given us a work like theirs, who sought only to place us in their position, that we might ourselves hear Him who spake as never man spake. Thus hath God chosen the foolish things of the world to confound the wise, and the weak things of the world to confound the things that are mighty.

CHAPTER VI.

NOTICES OF THE LIFE OF MATTHEW.

MATTHEW, called also Levi, was a Galilean, of the Jewish religion, and an inhabitant of Capernaum. His business was that of a publican, that is, a tax-gatherer; and he discharged the duties pertaining to that office at the lake of Galilee. It was an humble station, and among the Jews a despised one. Those who filled it were appointed by the Romans, to whom the Jews were now subject, and for whose use these taxes were collected. To pay tribute to them was not only a constant acknowledgment and badge of subjection and servitude, but to the Jews it was something more galling still. It wounded their religious as well as their patriotic pride. It was a thought of unmitigated bitterness, that the people of God should be held under the hated yoke of idolaters. The office itself being thus detestable, those who held and exercised it were universally scorned.

There were two orders, however, among the publicans,—the receivers-general, and their deputies. The former were usually selected from the higher classes of society, and were sometimes men of distinction. One of this order is named by Luke, xix. 2, who is called chief among the publicans, and a rich man. But the deputies were reckoned ignoble and contemptible even by the Gentiles themselves, and were, in fact, for the most part, rapacious and unmerciful men. Some one asked Theocritus which was the most cruel of all beasts. He answered, "Among the beasts of the wilderness, the bear and the lion; among the beasts of the city, the publican and the parasite." Members of this order are frequently classed in the Scriptures with sinners "Let him be unto thee as a heathen man and a sinner," is a phrase which expresses strongly the universal ban which was suspended over them. We are told, that, though a publican might be a Jew, he was hardly recognized as such by his countrymen. He was not allowed to enter the temple, nor to give testimony in courts of justice; and the very gifts which his devotion might prompt him to render were rejected from the altar of Jehovah as unclean and abominable.

Of this abhorred class, Matthew was a member. The duties of his office were discharged a little out of Capernaum, and by the shore of the lake of Galilee. Here his situation was such, that he soon learned whatever occurred in the adjoining country, to which the lake was a central place of business and resort. The fame of Jesus was not long in coming to his ears. Of his baptism on the banks of Jordan, of his sermon on the mount near Capernaum, and of the miracles which immediately followed, he had doubtless heard; and it is reasonable to suppose that he had resolved, that, as soon as a convenient opportunity allowed, he would unite himself with one whom so many things pointed out as the long-expected Messiah.

An opportunity was soon presented. Jesus, in going from Capernaum to some of the cities and villages on the shore of the lake, had occasion to pass by the place where the taxes were received, called in the Gospels *the receipt of custom*, and here, either having before heard of Matthew, or now receiving from his own lips a statement of his faith and wishes, the Saviour invites him to become his pupil and personal attendant. And Matthew arose, and left all, and followed him. We can but little imagine what his feelings must have been in that most eventful moment of his life. We can, however, most clearly see that this great step was taken from no worldly or selfish motive. For what was that Jesus to whom Matthew had now joined himself? He was without friends, without wealth, without home, without even a place where to lay his head. Matthew must have known that scorn and persecution would be the inevitable lot of all who should uphold the claims of the carpenter's son of Nazareth to be the long-expected Messiah, and that, in a worldly point of view, to relinquish for this lot his safe and doubtless lucrative publican's office, hateful though that was, would be but a poor exchange. There could have been, therefore, but one motive in Matthew's heart to lead to the great step in his life which he now proposed to take, and that motive was a sincere purpose to follow Him, however despised among men, who spake in his Father's name. Had it not been for that feeling in his heart, those few words, even from the Saviour's lips, "*Follow thou me*," would have fallen unheeded upon his ears. And so all invitations that now come to us, however affectionate and urgent they may be, will seem only like idle words, if we do not keep alive a tender feeling to which these may make appeal.

From this time forth Matthew abandons entirely his former business, and follows Jesus. He makes the act of doing this public; for on the day succeeding his call he prepares a supper at his house, to which he invites his new Master, and many publicans, his former associates. It was at this supper that many hypocritical Pharisees, passing by, exclaimed, "Why eateth your Master with publicans and sinners?" — Matthew ix. 11. They thought it was a strange and scandalous thing that one who set up as the Messiah of Israel, and the purifier of its ordinances, should take a publican to be a pupil, and should break bread — that greatest token of familiarity — with other publicans and sinners. And it was here that our Saviour made that ever-memorable reply, Matthew ix. 12, which has been well paraphrased in the following words: — "The religion which I came to teach embraces in its pure mercy the whole family of man; it draws no impassable line between the privileged and the profane; it leaves none to despair of Heaven's favor and acceptance; — if ye are perfect, if ye are whole, my errand is not to you; go; go to your temple, and perform your rites; but when there, study the meaning of that Scripture, 'I will have mercy and not sacrifice.' As for these, they are sick; they need a physician, and I must heal them; ye yourselves say that they are sinners, and why shall I not call them to repentance, and save them?"

Matthew says that all this was done "in the house" (Matt. ix. 10), without once intimating to whose house he referred. We learn from the other Gospels (Mark ii. 15, Luke v. 29), that it was in his own house that this feast was made and this conversation held. The humble publican had no desire to speak of himself, and it is remarkable that in his whole narrative he makes not the slightest allusion to himself, and even his name is but once mentioned. He records his own name in his catalogue of disciples (Matt. x. 2) and here he puts himself down as the eighth in the list, styling himself "Matthew the publican." Even in this we have an intimation of his character. Here was a proof of his humility and good-sense. Long after he had abandoned that despised calling, and had become a distinguished and honored man, he had no disposition to forget the station he had once held, nor was he ashamed to make it known. He cared not for the contempt which the confession might bring upon him. "He had the wisdom to perceive that there was no rank or occupation in life, however low, which could change the nature of true worth, or really disgrace an honest and virtuous man."

In all our Saviour's journeys, in all the scenes of his miracles, trials, sufferings, and death, we know not what particular part Matthew bore. We only know that he was a perpetual eyewitness and constant pupil. In that little band of disciples he seems never to have put himself forward, and never to have committed errors like those which brought remorse to the hearts of some of his brethren. He is never represented as taking part in conversations between the Saviour and his disciples, but maintains throughout the character of an humble, docile, and attentive learner.

The next notice we have of Matthew is after his Master had finished the great work of his mission, when the disciples, according to the last request of their Saviour, came together at Jerusalem. Matthew's name is expressly mentioned. Acts i. 13. Here he lived and taught, with his brethren, repeating to thousands of converts the same story of the life and words of Christ. In the persecutions that followed, when all the disciples were driven from Jerusalem, and were scattered abroad, it is not known to what place Matthew fled. Wherever he was, we may be sure he was employed, as were the other disciples, in preaching the glad news of the kingdom from city to city, and from house to house. In this work many years were diligently, but quietly, passed. Our next notice of him is about thirty years after the ascension of Christ, when we hear of him as having returned to the city of Jerusalem. It was here that he probably wrote out the Gospel which has always borne his name. After this, it is said that he travelled as a missionary into Parthia and Ethiopia, and that at Naddaber, a town in the latter country, he suffered a violent death rather than renounce his faith and hope in the Gospel of Christ. Thus, in the glorious company of the Apostles while living, he joined the noble army of the martyrs when dead.

CHAPTER VII.

THE GOSPEL OF MATTHEW.

FROM Matthew's life our attention is now to be directed to Matthew's Gospel. It was written, as has been said, at Jerusalem, and for the use of the churches in Judea. As a composition, it perfectly corresponds to what we have seen to be the character of its author. We see at once, upon reading this narrative, that the writer must have been a Jew, familiar with the opinions, ceremonies, and customs of his countrymen, conversant with the Old Testament writings, and habituated to their idiom. We see equally clearly, that he must have been a man of plain sense, of little or no learning, that he wrote seriously and from conviction, that he describes as an eyewitness, and without ever entertaining the most distant thought of setting off his narrative, or of introducing himself in it. As a composition intended to be read by the Jews, it is noticeable at once that this Gospel has less of those descriptions of places and customs, and definitions of Jewish words and phrases, which we shall find in the other Gospels that were written to be sent to Gentiles. By Matthew's readers all these things would be familiarly known. Such descriptions, for example, as are found in Mark vii. 3, or in John ii. 18, would be wholly uncalled for in Matthew's Gospel, and accordingly they are not found therein. The very word *Jew* or *Jews*, which occurs frequently in the other Gospels, is not used in Matthew. This proper noun, so likely to be employed by one writing at a distance from that people, would naturally be exchanged for some equivalent word by a writer in Judea; and accordingly

Matthew uses the words *multitude*, *people*, &c., in its stead. Moreover, in the selection of *materials* for this Gospel, there is a manifest choice of every circumstance which might conciliate the faith of the Jews. Thus, there was no opinion relating to the Messiah with which that people were more strongly impressed than this, that he must be of the race of Abraham and of the family of David. Matthew, therefore, with great propriety, begins his narrative with the genealogy of Jesus. He shows that *he* was of the seed of Abraham, and of the house of David. The Jews would have listened to no one's claims to be the Christ until this point had been proved. So, also, that the Messiah should be born at Bethlehem of Judea was another circumstance in which the learned Jews of those times were agreed. Micah v. 2. Matt. ii. 4. His birth in that city, with some memorable circumstances attending it, Matthew took the first opportunity to record. So, also, those passages in the prophets, or other sacred writers, which either foretell any thing that should occur to the Messiah, or admit an allusive application to him, are never passed over in silence by this Apostle. To the Jews, convinced of the inspiration of their sacred writings, the fulfilment of prophecy was always a great topic of argument. To the Gentiles, on the other hand, who knew nothing of the Old Testament predictions, this argument would be of but little force. Accordingly, in the other Gospels, designed, as we shall see, to be sent among the Gentiles, this argument is hardly ever adduced. But so great a weapon as this in controversy with the Jews, Matthew has frequently employed, and has hardly suffered an opportunity for its use to be neglected.

A few instances of this reference to the Old Testament may be named. In the minds of their readers it would have added but little to the effect of Mark's or Luke's account of

Christ's parables to have added, "All these things spake Jesus, that it might be fulfilled which was spoken by the prophet, saying, I will open my mouth in parables; I will utter things which have been kept secret from the foundation of the world." But Matthew gives this reference to the Old Testament (Matt. xiii. 35), and it was greatly to his purpose to do it, because the Jews thought these words predicted the manner in which their Messiah would teach.

Both Mark and Luke have recorded the fact, that before Christ entered upon his ministry he dwelt at Nazareth. But to their Gentile readers this fact furnished no proof that he was the Messiah. To the Jews, on the other hand, this was a proof; for they were familiar with a prophecy which said, "He shall be called a Nazarene." To that prophecy, Matthew, in recording the place where Jesus dwelt, has not failed to refer (Matt. ii. 23), and he alone has referred to it.

All the Evangelists write of the great number of the sick, of the lame, the dead, the possessed, whom Jesus restored with a word. That he wrought miracles was a proof of his divine mission to all alike, Gentiles and Jews; but that he wrought this particular class of miracles was a good argument in the mouth of Matthew alone, for his readers alone knew of the prophecy, "Himself took our infirmities, and bare our sicknesses," and this prophecy Matthew alone records. Matt. viii. 17.

At the crucifixion of Christ his garments were divided among the soldiers by lot. This all the Evangelists have related. It is Matthew alone who has added, "That it might be fulfilled which was spoken by the prophet, They parted my garments among them, and upon my vesture did they cast lots." Matt. xxvii. 35.

The more the peculiarities of each Gospel are studied, the more shall we be convinced that each of the writers drew up his own independent account. They could not have copied one from the other. Nor did their living and teaching together for so long a time destroy their individuality, and make one servilely repeat the other. When they sat down to write out their narratives, each one wrote freely, from his own independent remembrances, and with reference to the independent object which he had in view. And the adaptation of each Gospel to the particular object for which it was written is a proof of the great care which each bestowed upon its composition. Written with the utmost freedom and simplicity, still the Gospels were not written hastily nor carelessly. Their writers' hearts were too much in their work to permit that. Matthew no doubt felt tenderly for his brethren in the Jewish faith. The above are but a few instances where he betrays his affectionate solicitude to notice every circumstance that would operate to persuade them to admit the claims of Jesus to be their Christ.

But this did not lead him into an error of another kind. He was liable to the temptation of withholding altogether disagreeable truths, or, at least, of apologizing for them and softening them down. There is not the slightest trace of any yielding to this. When he comes to record facts disagreeable to the Jews, he does it with the utmost plainness and fearlessness. Thus, take the case of those terrible dooms which Jesus with such awful solemnity pronounced against the Scribes and Pharisees, the cities of Chorazin and Bethsaida, and even the Holy City, Jerusalem itself. Luke, writing to his Gentile friend Theophilus, very briefly repeats them as a part of the words of Christ; while Mark, thinking, doubtless, that they were intended for the Jews alone, and that they formed no part of that Gospel which was to be preached to all nations, has omitted them altogether. There may have been another reason which influenced this latter

Evangelist. At Rome, where Mark wrote, there was a disposition already too prevalent to insult and oppress the Jews, which Mark's repetition of these fearful denunciations might have needlessly increased. But Matthew has given them, every one of them, at length, and with the utmost distinctness and solemnity. Those awful decrees, uttered for *Jewish* ears, and intended for *their* warning, we all see that it was in Matthew's Gospel that they properly belonged, and there we find they are. It was not for the plain and fearless publican to shrink from making them known. It would have been no proof of a true affection to his brethren to have smoothed these things over. Their case required great plainness of speech, that they might be prepared for events, which, by all his confidence in Christ, he knew would come, and which, in fact, did come only a few years after he had written his Gospel. To be able to utter, with calmness and decision, truths which we know will provoke scorn and opposition, is one great mark of moral courage; and this virtue we must ascribe to Matthew.

Another peculiarity of this Gospel is, that it is the only one which was written in the very language which the Saviour used. The other Gospels were written in Greek, which was then a kind of universal language, as the French is now. Mark, Luke, and John, writing in this language, placed their histories within the reach of a much larger number of readers than if they had made use of any other tongue. But Matthew wrote for the Jews alone, and he wrote in their own language, the Hebrew. They understood the Greek, but this was the language that they loved. In the life of Paul, we read that on one occasion, when surrounded by a riotous multitude, they were stilled at once, and listened to him readily, when they perceived that he addressed them in the Hebrew tongue. And this is the language which the

Saviour used. We are reminded of this several times, by an occasional retention, in each of the Gospels, of a few original Hebrew words. Thus, when Jesus raised to life a young woman, he approached the bed where she lay, and said, *Talitha cumi*, which is to say, Damsel, I say unto thee arise. Mark v. 41. Again, when a man was brought to him who had an impediment in his speech, Jesus took up clay and touched his tongue, and, looking up to heaven, he said, *Ephphatha*, that is, Be opened. Mark vii. 34.

It at first seems unaccountable why the Evangelists should retain here the precise words of Christ. " They are not singular words. They are among the simplest, and admit without the least difficulty of being translated. Nay, they *are* translated in the very next breath. How shall we account for this curious feature in the narrative? It admits" — as it has been ingeniously suggested by Mr. Furness, in his Remarks on the Four Gospels, from which this quotation is made — " of an explanation which is wonderfully natural. Imagine the utterance of these simple words to have been instantly followed by the effects which they are said to have produced, namely, the restoration of the girl to life in the one case, and the recovery of the powers of hearing and speech in the deaf and dumb man in the other, and we perceive what stupendous power must have instantaneously passed, in the minds of those present, into those brief articulate sounds that issued from the lips of Jesus, and the utterance of which seemed naturally enough to be the cause of the astonishing effects produced. What peculiar, supernatural, and untranslatable significance must these words have instantly been thought to possess, which wrought or appeared to work so mightily! In the minds of the bystanders, those few sounds were instantly divorced, as by a stroke of lightning, from all familiar associations. Their ordinary import was lost in the new, instant, and unheard-of power which their utterance revealed. They no longer had any satisfactory correspondence with the articulations of any other language. No other forms of speech were felt to convey the same miraculous meaning, to possess the like force"; and when, years after, the Apostles sat down to recall and record those scenes, with what power of inexpressible associations did these very words press into their minds! What an impress of nature and reality do these mystic words impart to the narrative!

These remarks apply also to the Saviour's exclamation on the cross, *Eli, Eli, lama sabacthani?* that is to say, My God, my God, why hast thou forsaken me? Matt. xxvii. 46. No other words from mortal lips could express the associations which in the Apostles' minds were for ever linked to these words.

The Gospel of Matthew possesses peculiar interest, because it was at first drawn up entirely in the language which that Teacher uttered, who could attach such wonderful power to his words. It is true that the Gospel in that language has been lost. The most ancient form in which we now possess it is a translation into Greek, made soon after the original was composed. But there is no reason to doubt its exact faithfulness to the original. It was at once received by those who, reading familiarly both languages, would detect the slightest variation between the original and the translation. Though, then, we may be allowed to regret that we cannot look on the very words which this Apostle used in narrating the life and words of his Master, yet our faith need not be in the least disturbed by the loss, while there remains for us this translation of his history, so manifestly ancient, complete, and true.

One other circumstance, which gives peculiar value to the

Gospel of Matthew, may be named, and this is the remarkably clear and forcible style in which it is composed. Those who have much studied the peculiarities of the Evangelical narratives tell us that they could at once detect a paragraph of Matthew's history, if it were inserted in either of the other narratives. But it does not need any rare critical ex amination to appreciate the style of this writer. Let any one compare together Luke's and Matthew's record of the sermon on the mount, for example, and it will be at once seen how much superior in conciseness and energy is the latter. How observable especially is this in the manner in which each gives the beatitudes! Matt. v. 3-12, compared with Luke vi. 20-23.

The same simplicity and power of expression are found in the account Matthew gives of Christ's charge to his Apostles, his illustrations of the nature of his kingdom, and his replies to the cavils of his adversaries. It is for this reason that Matthew's Gospel has always been most highly esteemed, and has always been placed first in manuscript and printed collections.

We never feel more profoundly that our Gospel histories are true, than when we thus make a comparison, one with the other, to learn the object and peculiarities of each. The external evidence of their genuineness, that of manuscripts, and history, and tradition, is important; but there are marks in the Gospels themselves of honesty and truth, which, if only reflected upon, are far more convincing and satisfactory. There is a certain way of telling a story which be longs only to truth, and which, when perceived, carries with it all power of determining the understanding and touching the heart. But this way is perceived only by him who has sympathies with the truth, a free, open, and generous heart, that will discern it and bid it welcome. That famous aphorism of the Fathers, that all Scripture must be interpreted by the same spirit in which it was written, covers a great principle. We see it illustrated every day. To the coarse and uncultivated, what a mystery are the pleasures of a refined taste! to the selfish, how unintelligible are the impulses of generosity! how can the depraved and earthly conceive of the joys of devotion! One great reason why we are affected no more by the perusal of our Gospel histories is, that we have so little of that single-minded and all-devoted spirit in which they were written. Their authors had become like little children, in meekness, simplicity, reverence, and faith. Just in the proportion that we receive these virtues in our hearts shall we see in their writings signatures of honesty, sincerity, and reality, which we cannot resist, and which will draw us to Him in whom all treasures of wisdom are hid.

CHAPTER VIII.

NOTICES OF THE LIFE OF MARK.

In the twelfth chapter of the Acts of the Apostles, at the twelfth verse, we read these words: — "And Peter came to the house of Mary the mother of John, whose surname was Mark; where many were gathered together, praying." This is the first notice of Mark which we find in the Scriptures. We are here introduced to him in connection with an interesting incident in the life of that Apostle, with whom Mark afterwards long lived, and from whom he received the materials of the narrative which bears his name. Let us see what that incident was.

The family and friends of Mary had been filled with grief and fear, and they had come together to obtain the comfort and strength of prayer. The Apostle Peter, whom they had long known, honored, and loved, had been arrested by order of Herod, and had been thrown into prison, with the intention that he should soon be given up to be destroyed by the Jews. On the very night before he was to have been brought forth, he was found *sleeping* between two soldiers, — such is the tranquillity of an upright heart even in extreme danger. The account of his deliverance is given in Acts xii. 7; and we will observe to what place Peter, when freed, immediately directed his steps. He repaired at once to the house where a group of friends were offering their prayers to God for his release.

It is a circumstance which gives a great air of truth and reality to our Gospel histories, not only that individual characters are so well preserved, — such as the affectionate temper of John, the impetuous spirit of Peter, — but that we are occasionally presented with little groups of relatives and friends, who in those days, when all were exposed to persecution, would be so naturally drawn together. Thus the family of Lazarus, with his sisters Mary and Martha and their friends, forms one group, which with singular distinctness is presented before us. Then the women, Mary Magdalene, Mary the mother of James, Salome the wife of Zebedee, who attended the crucifixion, prepared spices to embalm the body, and were so early at the tomb after the ascension of Christ, form another group that was brought naturally and frequently together. Peter's house at Capernaum was a place where another like group of believers used to assemble, and there they had been sometimes favored with the presence and teachings of Christ.

Just such a place of assembling was this house of Mark's

mother, to which the released Apostle now approached. During his long residence in Jerusalem he had often been there, to instruct this family and their friends; and when they had heard of his arrest, they naturally came together, to sympathize with his fate, and to pray for his deliverance. And their prayer had been heard. So well was Peter known by them, that, when he stood at the door and knocked, his voice was at once recognized, and, as soon as their astonishment permitted them to attend to his words, he declared unto them how the Lord had brought him out of prison.

This, then, was the home of Mark, an inhabitant of Jerusalem, born and educated a Jew. He was not one of the twelve, nor a personal companion of Christ. At what time he embraced the new religion is not known, probably not until after the ascension of Christ. He was converted by Peter, who calls him his *son* (1 Peter v. 13), — a title which in those times was commonly given by the minister to every one who through him had been converted to the Christian faith. Doubtless this laid the foundation for that intimacy which we shall see always existed between the Apostle and his pupil.

Soon after Peter's release from prison, Mark determines to accompany Barnabas, who was his mother's brother, and Saul, in their journeys to preach the Gospel. It was at this time that he first took the surname of Mark, having been known before by the name of John. It was a practice with the Jews to assume names more familiar to the nations they visited than those by which they were known in their own country. Antioch was the first place to which Saul and Barnabas repaired, and from thence they were sent by the churches to Paphos, in the isle of Cyprus, and to Perga, in Pamphylia. Here Mark leaves these Apostles, and returns to his mother's house at Jerusalem. For what reason this step was taken, we have not been informed. It gave offence to Paul; for a few years after this, when he and Barnabas proposed another journey to visit and confirm the churches, and the latter was determined to take his nephew Mark with him, Paul, as we read in Acts xv. 38, " thought not good to take him with them, who departed from them at Pamphylia, and went not with them to the work. And the contention was so sharp between them, that they departed asunder one from the other," Barnabas taking Mark and sailing to Cyprus, while Paul, with Silas for a companion, departed through Syria and Cilicia.

How instructive is this account of the sharp contention, or *paroxysm*, as it is in the original, between these two distinguished disciples! We can imagine many reasons which induced Mark to return to his widowed mother at Jerusalem, reasons in themselves strong and satisfactory, which his mother's brother, Barnabas, would appreciate, but which, at the same time, might seem insufficient to one like Paul. He feared that Mark, if again employed, might desert them again; Barnabas, it is probable, knew that the causes which before called Mark home would not again exist; how natural, then, that this dispute, with men of such temperament as Paul and Barnabas, should wax warm, and lead to their separation! It proves that they were men,—just such men as we see now; and that their inspiration left them free to consult their own judgments, and to follow their own wills. It proves something more important still. The Gospel history, which they told from place to place, was no contrivance of theirs, which, as soon as they were vexed with one another and had separated, one of them would expose and renounce. When men plot some scheme of private interest or ambition, to impose upon the credulity of mankind under the cover of zeal for the public good, any contention or separation proves fatal to their undertaking, reveals their secret, and betrays their wicked design. Nothing like this occurred here, because nothing of a secret or private nature entered into the views of these men. When in their anger they separate, they go everywhere telling the same story, and teaching the same truths ; and thus we gain new evidence of the truth of the Gospel history even from the imperfections of its first teachers. Nor is this all. They not only prove it to be true historically, but they prove the influence its truth had upon their own hearts. Barnabas and Paul were men, and they separated in anger; but they were Christians, too, and they cherished no resentment. Paul had the magnanimity to retract his opinion, and to acknowledge his mistake in regard to the character of Mark. Not long after this dispute, we find that Paul had Mark with him as an esteemed fellow-laborer, and when again they were separated, the Apostle sends express word to Timothy, "Bring Mark with thee, for he is profitable to me for the ministry." — 2 Timothy iv. 11. Differences of opinion will often rise among men, and good men are not exempt from the weakness of advocating their own views with excess of positiveness and warmth. To cherish no resentment, to review one's opinion, and to acknowledge an error or mistake, — this is the Christian part, which the Apostles not only enjoined upon others, but acted themselves.

We must return to the life of Mark. His stay at Cyprus was not long. Barnabas, it is said, was soon stoned to death by the Jews residing on that corrupt and licentious island, and thus added another name to the great number of those who counted not their lives dear unto them for the sake of the Gospel of Christ. Mark, thus deprived of his companion and guide, sought out at once the Apostle Peter, the long and intimate friend of his family, his spiritual father, who better than any one else could further teach him the words of light and life. That Apostle, as is supposed, then dwelt at Antioch. Mark joins him there, and from this time remains with him, his constant attendant and assistant, we know not exactly how long, but probably for eight or ten years. The churches which Peter had especially under his care were those in Antioch, Pontus, Cappadocia, and Bithynia; and as the Christian history speaks of Mark as a fellow-traveller with Peter, they doubtless visited together these congregations of believers. After this we hear of Mark in Rome, for his name is affectionately mentioned at the conclusion of the epistles written from that city by Paul. Col. iv. 10. 2 Timothy iv. 11. Philemon 24.

It is the unanimous testimony of ancient writers, that Mark was entreated by the Christians of Rome to commit to writing what he had learned from Peter of the life and words of Christ. This was the occasion of the composition of his Gospel. When it was written, Mark travelled to Alexandria in Egypt, where he was the first to preach the new religion, and where he established a church. Here he soon died, and was buried.

Thus was secured another independent record of the life of Christ, from materials furnished by an eyewitness, and one of the most distinguished followers of the Saviour. Had it not been written then and there by Mark, Peter's independent and important testimony would not have been written at all. For this Apostle himself lived but a short time after Mark had been separated from him. In the eighth year of the cruel reign of Nero, both Peter and Paul were crucified, and thus they placed to the testimony they gave the seal of their blood. It is said, that, out of a feeling of humble respect for his Master, Peter requested to be crucified with his head downwards. "If so, it is an affecting conclusion of his eventful life, and another striking exhibition of the ardent character which adhered to him to the last. He conceived it too great an honor that such an one as he should meet his death erect, and looking upwards, like his beloved and venerated Lord; and so, with his head in the dust, he closed his labors, his failings, his victories, his sufferings, and his life."

These occasional notices of Peter's life seem to have been called for in connection with that of Mark, because the Gospel of Mark comes to us on the authority of Peter. For this reason, it has sometimes been called the Petrine Gospel; but, as it was written by his companion and pupil, the title which it has always borne in our Bibles is evidently the proper one.

CHAPTER IX.

THE GOSPEL OF MARK.

From all we know of Mark, it is very evident that both he and his family occupied a humble position in society. In all his journeys with Barnabas and Paul, and with Peter, he is named only as *their* minister,—as high a station, doubtless, as he desired, or for which his education qualified him. Now with all this his Gospel remarkably corresponds. Its language is more like the language of an uneducated man than that of any other writing which the New Testament contains. It is less copious, more harsh, more abounding in expressions that are unusual and barbarous to the tongue. He describes clearly; we have no difficulty in understanding his meaning; but every thing is narrated with great brevity, and with a baldness and awkwardness of expression which will be seen on comparing his narrative with that of Matthew or Luke.

Another peculiarity of this Gospel is, that, although written in Greek, and written, too, by one who in every chapter proves himself a Jew, we still find Roman, that is Latin, names and words, which occur in no other Gospel, and which sound oddly in the midst of words of a different tongue. Thus the other Evangelists, in writing of the title *centurion*, captain of a hundred men, make use of the common Greek word that denoted that office. Mark, on the other hand (xv. 19), designates it by the word by which it was always called among the Romans. The mere English reader will not perceive the difference, which is seen at once in the original. So, in Mark xii. 42, the value of the sum which the poor widow cast into the treasury is expressed by naming a Roman coin. Again, in Mark vii. 4, which contains an account of the Jewish ceremony of washing hands before meat, to the vessel made use of for this purpose Mark gives not the common name applied to it by the Jews, but one more familiarly known by the Romans. If in using these words Mark had no design to make himself better understood by those for whose benefit he was writing, we all know how unconsciously just such words as the above, if they have been recently used, will at once occur to the memory of the speaker or writer, even though using for the moment a different tongue.

A more remarkable peculiarity of this Gospel may be found in the frequent explanations of places and customs which Mark introduces, in order to be better understood by his readers at Rome. Thus, when he has occasion to mention the Jordan (Mark i. 5), he prefixes the explanation *the river*, an explanation needed only in a distant country. The word translated *hell* in our New Testaments is literally the name of a place near Jerusalem, the valley of Hinnom, where infants had been sacrificed by fire to Moloch; a place well known to the inhabitants of Judea, but of which the Romans were ignorant. Accordingly, Mark, when he mentions it, adds, *the fire that never shall be quenched.* Mark ix. 43, 45. The Jews applied the word *corban* to property which any man set apart to the exclusive service of God. Ungrateful and impious children, who had aged and infirm parents, would make *corban* of their property, and thus avoid their support. The Saviour reproved them for thus making null the commandments of God through their tradition. In giving an account of this, Mark uses the word *corban*, but he fails not to define it, — a gift to the Lord of that by which thou mightest have been profited by me, — without which explanation to his readers, this reproof of the Saviour would be entirely misunderstood. Mark vii. 11. In the second verse of that same chapter, the phrase "*defiled* hands" would probably have suggested to Roman ears some offence more heinous than neglect of a superstitious washing, had not Mark taken pains so to define it. Two remarkable verses follow, in these words: — "For the Pharisees, and all the Jews, except they wash their hands oft, eat not, holding the tradition of the elders. And when they come from the market, except they wash, they eat not. And many other things there be which they have received to hold, as the washing of cups and pots, and brazen vessels, and of tables."

That Mark was writing for the benefit of other than Jewish readers must be obvious from this example alone. But there is another remark to be made in respect to the foregoing quotation. So much of mere comment and explanation from the writer is nowhere else to be found in the Gospels. This single fact is a proof how little these writers ever speak in their own names. They always retire behind the facts they record, anxious that you should look at these alone. It is this circumstance which makes this long comment of Mark noticeable; and at first we may wonder why he should have put it forward. But when we read on a little farther, what do we find? That Mark immediately gives the long sermon of Christ, in which he shows that there is but one thing that can truly defile a man, namely, his own evil heart. A moment's study of the passage leads us to see that the whole force of this sermon depends upon a knowledge of this Jewish custom, which was the text and explanation of the discourse. The Saviour's doctrine would not have been comprehended, if the contrast which he draws between ceremonial washing and inward purity had not been preserved. This instance, requiring him to step so far aside from his usual way of narration, is a striking one of Mark's great care to adapt his Gospel to the comprehension of those for whose benefit it was composed.

We see the same care, also, in the selection of the materials for his Gospel. Mark, doubtless, had knowledge, through the Apostle Peter, of all the important events in the life of Christ. But many facts which we find in Matthew are wholly omitted in Mark. The reason is, he knew they would be of less consequence to his readers at Rome. Of this character were the genealogy of Christ, notices of his parents, the time and circumstances of his birth, of the very place of which — the little town of Bethlehem — probably the most of these at Rome had never heard. All these particulars Mark properly passes by. For the same reason is another fact, before noticed, that Mark gives us in a few words the discourses against the Scribes and Pharisees.

There is one other observation respecting Mark's Gospel, which suggests a peculiarly interesting light in which to survey it. If it was composed of materials furnished to Mark by Peter, we shall naturally expect to find *Peter* in it, that is to say, traces of his independent knowledge and of his peculiar character.

Such traces are found. We shall be able to notice only a few of the many particulars upon which the testimony of Peter in this Gospel throws a new and important light. The conduct of our Saviour, when he was told that his mother and his brethren stood without, desiring to speak with him, appears singular and unnatural in Matthew's account of it. Matt. xii. 48. The Saviour gave no attention to their request, and does not appear to have noticed them. In Mark, a circumstance unrecorded by the other writers is added, which explains and justifies the course which Jesus took. We are here told, that " his kinsmen went out to lay hold on him; for they said, He is beside himself." Mark iii. 21. Jesus, therefore, knew what they wanted of him, and would not permit their false view to interrupt him.

Matthew, Mark, and Luke record, that, as Jesus was going to be crucified, the soldiers compelled one Simon, a Cyrenean, to bear the cross. In Mark's Gospel alone we read that this Simon was the father of Alexander and Rufus. Mark xv. 21. Why should Mark have added this fact? Because, as we incidentally learn from the Epistle to the Romans, Rufus was then living in Rome. Romans xvi. 13. That the Saviour's cross was borne by the father of one then living in that city was a fact interesting to Mark's readers, and to his alone. It is probable that Peter, in narrating the crucifixion of his Master to his Roman hearers, often referred to this Rufus, then living among them, as one who could testify that his own father was a witness and an unwilling abetter of that awful scene. A man, conscious that every word he uttered could be confirmed, would naturally make such an appeal as this to a present witness; and here is an instance of a coincidence between the Gospels and the Epistles, which must have been undesigned, and which, as we should acknowledge were we legally examining these documents, casts a convincing light on the question of their authenticity.

We find, also, in this Gospel, traces of Peter's peculiar character. This Apostle was one of the most distinguished companions of Christ, who was at times both commended and severely reproved by his Master. In giving an account to Mark of the life and words of Jesus, Peter must often speak of himself, and a man will betray his character by the manner in which he does this. What accounts, then, of Peter do we find in this Gospel of Mark? Precisely the same accounts that we find in the Gospels of Matthew and Luke. It is the same Peter in all; the same bold, over-confident, impulsive, denying, yet quickly repentant and deeply affectionate disciple. The facts stand in all their bald simplicity in this Gospel, just as they stand in the others. Peter puts in not one word of explanation, not one whisper of apology or palliation. In relation to that event which was so full of unmitigated grief and remorse, the denial of his Master, it is Peter's own account of it that makes us most deeply feel its folly and its guilt. The circumstances that preceded it, the prediction of Jesus that Peter would forsake him, and the solemn assurance of the Apostle that he would not, are related with more distinctness and impressiveness in Mark's Gospel than in either of the others. The reason how natural! Those were words which sunk deep into Peter's heart, which he never forgot, and which, though they told such an awful tale against him, it was not for him to suppress.

Generous and devoted disciple! With all the weaknesses and sins into which he was betrayed, who of us does not love him? How can we lay up any thing against any human being, however erring and sinful, who, only by a *look* of reproval, is made to go out and weep bitterly?

While, then, Peter keeps not back an account of that bitter rebuke, does it appear that he was equally forward to make mention of the praise which he received from his Master's lips? Here, too, we have an indication of character both beautiful and delicate. You remember those emphatic words of Jesus, pronouncing Peter blessed, declaring him to be the rock of the church, and to possess the keys of heaven. You remember it was supposed that these words conferred some preëminence upon Peter, and that therefore they created offence in the little band of equal disciples. You will find these words in the Gospel of Matthew. Matt. xvi. 17–19. They are not found in the Gospel of Mark. The occasion on which they were uttered is named, and other conversation which was then held is narrated. Mark viii. 27–29. The words of praise are not repeated; and yet could Peter have forgotten them?

Thus, in reading our four Gospel histories, there is hardly any thing with which we may be more deeply impressed, than with the fact that their writers must have been themselves influenced by the doctrines which they taught. These doctrines, the veriest infidel allows, are adapted to make men love honesty, sincerity, and truth. So far, then, as we see that they had effect upon those who taught them, so far must we also see the moral impossibility that these men could all the while be engaged in a dark work of forgeries and lies. Who is credulous enough to believe that? By all that their Master taught them they were made humble, forgetful of themselves, indifferent to the world's favor or reproach, in love only with the truth; they were holy men, and could not speak otherwise than as they were moved by the spirit of sincerity and truth.

CHAPTER X.

NOTICES OF THE LIFE OF LUKE.

THESE are but few, and for the most part unsatisfactory. The author of two important books, the Gospel and the Acts of the Apostles, Luke had the self-forgetfulness so characteristic of the first disciples, who did not deem any thing relating to their own history worthy the slightest notice in connection with Him whose life and words they were called to record. Luke has never, in either of his histories, mentioned himself by name. In giving an account of Paul's labors and travels, whose companion and assistant Luke was, he yet says no more of the part which he acted than such expressions as these imply: — "*we* journeyed," "*we* sailed," "*we* abode." Paul, in his epistles, makes occasional allusion to Luke by name, and from these sources, and from what we learn from credible historians, almost contemporaneous, we gather the materials for the following sketch.

He was born in Antioch, about fifteen years before the birth of Christ. Of the converts made to the new religion in the age of the Apostles, he was the oldest of whom we have any account. Antioch was at this time one of the most celebrated cities of the East, the capital of Syria, and the residence of the Roman governors. Here all religions were tolerated, and the population was composed of Greeks, Romans, Macedonians, and Jews. Luke was born, it is probable, of Gentile parents. Paul, in his Epistle to the Colossians (iv. 14), implies that he was not of the circumcision, as he gives his name after the names of those whose Jewish descent is expressly affirmed. See Col. iv. 7–11. He doubtless received a Gentile education, and was trained up to the profession of a physician. He was, therefore, a man of some learning. Those who followed this profession received more instruction than most men, both in their particular art and in general literature. They obtained, besides, that practical knowledge which may be acquired by an extensive intercourse with society. These qualifications were not of a low order, it is likely, in a city so learned as that of Luke's birthplace, where the Greek language in its purity had long prevailed, and letters had long been cultivated, and where people of the first distinction resided. At what time Luke was made a convert to the Jewish religion is not known. It is probable he became such early in life, as throughout his Gospel and the Acts he shows the utmost familiarity with its doctrines and ceremonies, with the language of its sacred books, and with places and customs of Judea.

Here, then, at Antioch, Luke lived, as is supposed, until he was about fifty years of age, discharging the duties of his profession, and enjoying his religion as a proselyte Jew. Meantime all the events had been transpiring, in the neighbouring province of Judea, of which we read in the Gospels, — the birth of the Saviour, his baptism, his ministry, his wonderful works, his arrest, trial, crucifixion, resurrection, and ascension; and how worthy of our notice is it that God should now raise up, in this enlightened city of Antioch, another historian of all these facts, in the person of such a man as Luke, — a man of age and attainments, whose character was well formed and was probably well known!

Of the time and manner in which Luke first became acquainted with the Gospel, we have not been informed. We know clearly only what he has told us in the preface to his Gospel, that he was not an eyewitness of the events of the Saviour's life, but obtained a knowledge of them from those who were eyewitnesses and ministers of the word; and also what we learn from the Acts, that, soon after Paul's conversion, Luke joined that Apostle, as his companion and assistant. It seems probable that Luke was converted to the Christian faith on the day of Pentecost. This was an oocasion, when, as a Jewish believer, he would naturally be present at Jerusalem; and what more probable than that he was one of the great number of devout persons, out of every nation, who had then come together in that city? Here, convinced by the miracles which on that day converted three thousand to the Christian faith, he made this the subject of his careful inquiry, and availed himself of all opportunities to hear the preachers of the new religion. During the years they spent in Jerusalem, Luke lived with them, as we have reason to conclude, and took part himself in their work of repeating to others the story of the life and words of Christ. Thus we see the sources of his information, and how his narrative also became influenced by the style of the Apostle's oral accounts.

We now pass several years down the course of events. The Apostles had fulfilled their ministry in Jerusalem, according to His word who told them to tarry for a time in that city, their number had been greatly enlarged, and that bold and able advocate, Paul of Tarsus, had been raised up to their cause. The martyrdom of Stephen and the imprisonment of Peter were soon followed by days of persecution, that separated the Apostles and early preachers from one another, and sent them everywhere abroad as missionaries of the new faith. In this dispersion Paul went to Antioch, to which place Luke had before repaired. Here the acquaintance between the Apostle and Evangelist probably commenced. Here Paul established a church, of which Luke was, doubtless, a prominent member. It was in this city, also, and at this time, that the disciples were first called Christians. Acts xi. 26.

Not long after this, we find that Luke has determined to devote himself to the work of spreading a knowledge of these glad tidings abroad in the world. What the young disciple Mark did when he connected himself with Peter, what Matthew the publican did when the Saviour met him at the receipt of custom, this the older and more experienced Luke now does, — he leaves all to follow the call of Christ. So strong was the sense of duty in the hearts of these men! They broke away from every attachment of kindred and country and habit and home, that they might everywhere bear witness to what they knew was for the healing and salvation of the world. In the case of Luke, this is particularly remarkable. He had now reached a period in life when men oftener think of retiring from its cares, than of turning their feet to a new and perilous pursuit. The fervors of youth had passed away, and all his tastes and attachments must have confined him, in his declining years, to the city where he was born, and where for so long a time he had followed the duties of his profession. But all these he now overcomes, and joins himself, as a companion and fellow-laborer, to the Apostle Paul.

We have before seen how natural it was that Peter and Mark should unite together in their labors as missionaries and preachers of the word. They both sprang from the same humble station in life, they had for a long time been previously acquainted with one another, they had sustained to each other the relation of teacher and pupil. Equally natural was it that two such men as Paul and Luke should unite together as companions and fellow-laborers. The former was brought up at the feet of Gamaliel, and was learned in the wisdom of the ancients, and in the sacred books of the Jews; the latter, likewise, from education, profession, and the intercourse of his whole life with intelligent society, was a man of considerable attainments, accustomed to close examination and careful thought. Among all the early converts to the new religion, we know of no other one like these two men. How natural, then, that they should labor together, to bear one another's burdens and to help one another's joys!

Luke was with Paul, more or less, for many years. The account of their journeys, preachings, and many trials, he has recorded in the book of the Acts. It is evidence of the great minuteness and exactness with which he has done this, that, with a common ancient map before us, we can trace the course of their voyages, see the islands at which they touched, and the places where they preached. In all these perils and labors, what particular part Luke himself bore we can only conjecture. It is noticeable that Paul does not call Luke his minister, as he did Mark. Luke was a fellow-laborer, an equal, the beloved physician,— one on whose wisdom and experience Paul leaned for support. Paul was younger, more active, a more gifted, and a more remarkable man, whose education, habits, wonderful conversion, and bold temperament qualified him to be prominent in action and address. Such he appears throughout the narrative; it is of what Paul said, and did, and suffered, that Luke chiefly speaks. Luke himself was declining in years, from the habits of his profession he was unused to public harangues, and although in his modesty he has hardly said a word of himself, we know at least this much, that he minutely observed and carefully recorded every thing that came under his notice, that he was Paul's judicious, confidential counsellor, and steady and supporting friend.

With the imprisonment of Paul at Rome, the history in the book of Acts concludes. Here, also, terminate Luke's incidental notices of his own life. The most credible account which has been handed down of the remaining part of the life of this Evangelist leads us to conclude that he soon left Rome and settled in Greece. It is said that he here wrote his Gospel and the Acts, and soon after died, at the venerable age of eighty-four.

CHAPTER XI.

THE GOSPEL OF LUKE.

From these brief notices of the life of Luke, we are now to turn to the Gospel which bears his name. We are struck at once with the manner in which he begins his narrative, it is so different from that of the other Evangelists. According to the taste of the Greeks and Romans, which he doubtless acquired in his Gentile education, he opens his history with a preface, from which we learn his intentions in writing, the sources of his knowledge, and the name of the person for whose benefit the work was undertaken. It is a long, carefully written, and well-balanced sentence, of pure and well-chosen words. How would it have sounded, had it been placed at the beginning of the narrative of Matthew or of Mark! Neither of them appears to have given a thought to the selection of language, or to have cared any thing for style. Luke's preface is appropriate to no place but to that where it is. Here it is in perfect keeping with the man.

The title "most excellent" was bestowed upon those who held offices of considerable importance under the Roman emperors, such offices as superintendents of sacred edifices, overseers of public revenue, deputy governors in the provinces; and as Luke gives geographical notices of places not in the neighbourhood of Greece, it is probable that Theophilus resided in that country, and was some distinguished man converted and instructed by Luke, when he went there to spend the few last years of his old age. The following are references, in Luke's Gospel, to descriptions which would have been unnecessary had he been writing to one well acquainted with Judea: i. 26; iv. 31; viii. 26; xxiii. 51; xxiv. 13. So, too, in the Acts, we find that places in Judea and in Asia Minor are named as if they were less known than those in Greece and those between Greece and Rome, with which a public officer of Greece would naturally be acquainted. These facts sufficiently indicate the residence of Theophilus.

One other thing in this preface deserves our notice, as it throws light upon the state of feeling which then existed in regard to the Christian religion. Luke mentions, as one reason why he wrote his Gospel, that *many* had taken in hand to give account of the Saviour's life and words. Had these accounts been entirely trustworthy and satisfactory, his own labor would have been unnecessary. No doubt these were brief and contradictory relations. Of course, he does not refer to the Gospels of Matthew, Mark, and John. He would not so allude to the narratives of three writers, two of whom had better opportunities of information than himself, while the other had opportunities equally as good. Besides this,

John's Gospel was not at this time written, while the Gospels of Matthew and Mark, if then composed, of which there is much reason to doubt, were published in countries remote from Greece, and were not then, it is probable, familiarly known.

There were, then, other, but imperfect, accounts of Christ's life and words, known in Greece before Luke prepared his Gospel. How natural that such accounts should have existed! Thirty years had elapsed since the events of the Saviour's life transpired in Judea. A knowledge of them must have been carried to all parts of the world by Jews and others. What could have been more natural than that brief, incorrect, and contradictory accounts of events so wonderful should have been frequently committed to writing, and that they should awaken much curiosity, and should be sought after by persons of various descriptions? The fact named by Luke is of much importance, as it shows that the Christian religion attracted the attention of mankind at the very time when its pretensions could be easily exposed if they were false. Our Gospels were not presented to the world at a time when an absolutely dead indifference prevailed as to their contents. They had acquired no sanction of age, nor had opportunities to test their authenticity passed by, before their merits were discussed. On the contrary, at the very time they were written, men were asking what might be depended upon for truth. They were composed and published for this very purpose, to distinguish and preserve what was certain and worthy of reliance. And time, that trieth all things, has consigned to oblivion those accounts of the *many*, to which the occurrence of marvellous events always gives birth, and which were doubtless written in haste and from mere rumor, while it has safely handed down to us the carefully written narratives of those who embalmed their words in the ever-living spirit of deep sincerity and truth.

Of Luke's Gospel as a book, the most striking peculiarity is the great research which it betrays, and the surprising care, precision, and fulness of detail with which it is written. Luke tells us that he had accurately informed himself of all things from the beginning (i. 3); and that he had taken great pains to do this is evident throughout. Indeed, Luke appears to have been a man who heartily loved dates, and names, and a statement of facts. A trait of character like this rarely belongs to such men as Matthew and Mark; but how very natural to find it in the old age of a man who had long followed that profession which, more than any other, creates habits of observing and recording facts! A quotation of a verse or two from his Gospel will illustrate this trait of his character. It is found at the beginning of the third chapter. "Now in the fifteenth year of the reign of Tiberius Cæsar, Pontius Pilate being governor of Judea, and Herod being tetrarch of Galilee, and his brother Philip being tetrarch of Iturea and of the region of Trachonitis, and Lysanias the tetrarch of Abilene, Annas and Caiaphas being the high-priests, the word of God came unto John, the son of Zacharias, in the wilderness." Could any man take greater pains to insure precision and fix a date? He wishes to settle the precise time when a certain man began to preach; he tells his name, the name of his father, the neighbourhood where he first appeared, who were high-priests at the time, the name of the offices and of the officers of the three highest civil stations in the country, the name of the emperor who ruled over all, and the very year of his reign.

The same love of preciseness in recording facts is seen in the other book of this Evangelist, the Acts of the Apostles. Thus, on one occasion, he gives account of his accompanying Paul, then a prisoner, on his way to Rome. Acts xxvii. 1. They sail from Tyre under the care of Julius, a centurion, belonging to the band of Augustus; the vessel was owned at Adramyttium, and Aristarchus, a Macedonian of Thessalonica, was a fellow-passenger. The day after they launched, they touched at Sidon, sailed near the island of Cyprus, over the sea of Cilicia, and landed at Myra, a city of Lycia. All this is within the compass of five verses. Look at another extract from his journal. Acts xxviii. 11. They had been shipwrecked upon the island of Malta. They were obliged to remain here three months. They then obtained passage in a ship belonging to Alexandria; her name was Castor and Pollux; she had wintered at the isle. They soon landed at Syracuse; here they stopped three days. They then beat their way against opposing winds to Rhegium, where they remained one day; then, a south wind blowing, they passed on towards Rome.

This unusual minuteness in recording so many little facts, names, and places sprung from no design to accumulate evidence of the truth of his history; still less was it an appeal, which, so often made, might have seemed vain and ostentatious, to hundreds of witnesses of his veracity, who might have then been found. Luke writes as if he never once thought that his statements would be called in question. Every thing is put down naturally, as the record of a very observing man, whose habit and delight it was to preserve all connected facts. It is true that every additional circumstance he mentions furnished to his readers a new test of his credibility, but there is nowhere the slightest indication that Luke for a moment thought of this. Impressed with the reality of every thing he relates, he betrays no consciousness that it had ever occurred to him that his narrative could appear otherwise than as simple and consistent reality to any body. Accordingly, throughout his writings, as indeed throughout the writings of the other Evangelists, there is a quiet, unobtrusive confidence in his narrative, which could have sprung only from the profoundest conviction of its truth.

To these traits of Luke's character which have now been noticed, to his spirit of research, and love of minuteness, and precision in recording facts, we are very largely indebted. They led him to gather up and preserve many interesting particulars, of which the other Evangelists leave us uninformed. Thus the beautiful hymn of Mary before the birth of Jesus (Luke i. 46), Zacharias's song of thanksgiving when he named his son John (Luke i. 67), and the devout address of good old Simeon in the temple (Luke ii. 29), are given by Luke alone. We may suppose that these words were written out in full afterwards by these persons, as descriptive of what they felt and imperfectly expressed on the above-named occasions, and that Luke, when in Judea, obtained copies of them, and inserted them in their place near the beginning of his Gospel. Had it not been for his care, they would not have been preserved.

So, also, no one can compare the Gospels together, without at once seeing how many more parables Luke gives than any of the other Evangelists. Those simple and most beautifully wrought allegories, — that of the rich man and Lazarus, the prodigal son, the Pharisee and the publican, the good Samaritan, — are found in Luke alone. Matthew and Mark did all that the necessities of the occasions that gave rise to their Gospels required or permitted; the absence of these parables from their narratives does not surprise us. But how well does it comport with all that we know of the taste and character of Luke, that, in his journeys in Judea and conversations with the Apostles, he should treasure up these parables with minutest care, and that when he wrote, in the leisure of his old age, he should take so much pains to record them in full! Thus it is through him that these divine lessons have given so much delight and wisdom to the world.

To the same care of Luke in observing and recording facts, we owe a knowledge of many other particulars,—those relating to the birth of John, the occasion of Joseph's being in Bethlehem when Jesus was born, the vision granted to the shepherds who watched their flocks by night, the journey of the child Jesus when twelve years old to Jerusalem, the conversion of Zaccheus the publican, the repulse the Saviour and his disciples met when about to enter a Samaritan city, the instructive rebuke he then gave to two of his disciples for their intemperate zeal, the mission of the seventy, and the affecting interview during the walk to Emmaus. All these are recorded in the Gospel of Luke alone.

And yet it is worth our while to observe that this Evangelist, with all his minute attention to facts, sometimes makes most indefinite allusions to time and place in narrating the events of successive days in the life of Christ. Thus he has occasionally phrases like these,—"*in a certain city*," "*at a certain village*," "*on one of those days*," "*at that season*," &c., referring to times and places which are more exactly designated in the Gospel of Matthew. Compare Luke v. 12 with Matt. viii. 2; also, Luke xv. 1 with Matt. ix. 10. The obvious conclusion is, that Luke had not seen Matthew's Gospel. If he had, he would have been glad to learn the exact time and place from that Evangelist. How well does this different method of indicating the succession of events agree with what we have seen to be the origin of these two Gospels! Luke, who received the history from the Apostles, as they preached on different occasions, for different purposes, and without regard to chronological order, was as minute and precise in his facts as he could be, but was necessarily less exact in some matters of time and place than Matthew, who knew when and where the events transpired, because he was an eyewitness of their occurrence.

It has been before remarked, that we see the influence of Luke's Gentile education in prefixing to his Gospel a formal preface, so much after the taste of the Roman and Greek authors. We see the same thing in his marking events by the reign of the Roman emperor, or of Roman governors, — such as the birth of John, the birth of Christ, and the time when the Baptist began his ministry. We see the same thing, also, in the genealogy which Luke has given. Matthew, writing for Jews, traces the line from Abraham and David down to Christ, in order to prove that the ancient prophecies of a Messiah were fulfilled in him. But it was no part of Luke's object to prove this, because the Gentile Theophilus knew nothing of those prophecies. Accordingly, he gives a genealogy after the Gentile manner, ascending from the person whose lineage is given, upward to the founder of his family. Thus he entirely reverses the order of Matthew. These genealogies have been a great cause of perplexity to all commentators. On comparing them together, we find that there are discrepancies between them. We cannot doubt that they were copied from family records, in keeping of which the Jews have ever been scrupulously exact, and that, whatever errors may have crept into their frequent transcription since, they were originally correct. Else they would have been attacked, as they were not, by early Jewish and infidel opponents. The more common way of explaining these discrepancies is by supposing that several intermediate names have been dropped from the list of Matthew; and that, when Luke says that Joseph was the son of Heli (iii. 23), he means an adopted son, a son-in-law. Then Luke gives the pedigree of Mary's line, as Matthew gives that of Joseph's.

The influence of Luke's education is seen again throughout his Gospel in his style, structure of sentences, and use of words. His sentences are longer, more involved, and elaborated. He has a more copious use of words; and although he sometimes adopts harsh Hebrew expressions, borrowed, no doubt, from his intercourse first with the Jews and then with the Apostles, yet his language generally is pronounced to be the purest Greek which the New Testament contains, and shows that he had been trained to a correct knowledge and careful use of that tongue. Traces have been found in his writings, it is thought, of his medical profession. Thus in Luke iv. 38 he distinguishes a fever by words employed by old medical writers, while in Acts xiii. 11 he uses a technical word for blindness.

In Luke's Gospel, therefore, we do not see so much of one kind of simplicity, — simplicity of language, — as we see in the Gospels of Matthew and Mark. In a man of Luke's education and life this could not exist. But we see just as much of another kind of simplicity, — simplicity of design, simplicity of heart. He had the same object before him that the other Evangelists had, — to record the life and words of Christ; and as with them, so with him, this great object engrossed all attention. He himself is as nobody. He introduces nothing as coming from himself, no opinions, no conjectures, no reasonings, no inferences, no surprise, no admiration. In the language in which he had been educated, and with the minute accuracy of taste and habit, he gives nothing but the naked facts.

These facts he transmitted to his friend Theophilus, that

he might know the certainty of the things in which he had been instructed. This Gospel was God's message to him. None the less is it God's message to us, that, by studying its words, pondering its truths, obeying its instructions, and imbibing its spirit, we also may know the *certainty* of these things. And their certainty we may know. We cannot, indeed, go to the places which this Evangelist so minutely describes, nor inquire of the men with whom he journeyed. These are tests of his credibility which in their very nature are not perpetual, though by these his words were once tried, and they have abided. But there are other tests than these outward ones of the senses, by which we may determine, and by which alone, after all, we can determine, what is true and right and good. We have the test of our reason and conscience and heart. Let us bring the Gospel message home to a personal trial and proof. We shall then have the witness in ourselves. For our guide in life, our help in weakness, our comfort in sorrow, our support in death, it is God's precious gift to us, and that by which the secrets of all hearts shall at last be judged.

CHAPTER XII.

NOTICES OF THE LIFE OF JOHN.

WE come now to the life of one whose character is distinguished at once from that of all the other followers of Christ, and betrays itself in almost every verse of his writings. Mild and affectionate, faithful and confiding, a double portion of the Saviour's spirit seems to have rested upon him; and hence what a peculiar tie connected the Teacher and the pupil together! Jesus was loved by John with a love which only John's deep heart could offer him, while John was the disciple whom Jesus loved.

Notices of his life are more clear and satisfactory than those pertaining to the other Evangelists. Matthew, Mark, and Luke all tell us that John was the son of Zebedee and Salome, that he lived in Bethsaida, — a little fishing town on the northern shore of the lake of Galilee, — and was brought up to his father's business, which was that of a fisherman. This was the common occupation of those who lived near that lake; and although it was an humble employment, it nevertheless appears, from various incidental notices, that John's father was not destitute of property, nor in a low condition of life. When called to be a disciple, we read that John left hired servants in the ship with his father. Mark i. 20. John appears always to have had a home of his own, to which he received Mary, the mother of his Lord, when she was commended to his care. John xix. 27.

By his mother John was related to Christ, and by no distant connection. Salome was a daughter of Joseph, born to him with other children before his espousal to Mary, the mother of Jesus. Hence Salome was reckoned our Lord's sister, and John was his nephew. This relationship explains several circumstances in this Gospel, and it is important, therefore, that it be borne in mind. It gives us reason to suspect that John was early acquainted with Jesus. He, living with his parents at Nazareth, was but a few miles distant from John, following his father's business on the lake. Being related, no doubt their families sometimes met, and thus John can hardly be supposed to have been ignorant of all the wonderful events preceding and following the birth of Christ, such as the appearance of the angel to his mother, the visit of the Magi at Bethlehem, the mysterious and deeply pondered words said of him when he was presented in the temple, the divine communications that directed his flight into Egypt, and his ever memorable visit, when twelve years old, to Jerusalem. Events in themselves so wonderful, and so clearly showing that a peculiar providence was watching over Jesus, and was preparing him for some high work, must have been well known to near relatives, all of whom were then looking for the consolation of Israel; and very naturally did they lead the mind of John to determine upon the course he pursued. He resolved to improve the first favorable opportunity that presented to connect himself with Jesus, that by intercourse with him he might be prepared for that new order of events which it was so clear God was soon to establish. That opportunity was near at hand. Jesus had been baptized, and had passed through the scene of his temptation, and while on his way from Capernaum to visit the villages of Galilee, he came to the lake, where he saw the two brothers, James and John, in a ship with their father, mending their nets. Upon invitation, they left the ship and followed Jesus. John was the fourth one now added to the number of disciples, and we are told that he was the youngest of the twelve.

It is impossible, as has been beautifully said by Dr. Greenwood, in his Lives of the Apostles, that either John or his brother could have dreamed of the consequences to which the step they had now taken would lead. "Hitherto it had been their only care to rise up, day by day, to the contented exercise of their humble toil, to ply their oars, to spread their sails, to cast their nets, and to dispose of their freight in their native village or in the neighbouring towns, for the support of themselves and their families." The scene just around them, the peaceful lake, the surrounding hills, their own low-roofed dwellings, looking out kindly upon them, and containing all that they loved,—this was their little world. Here they lived as their fathers lived before them; and here, hoping for the long-promised deliverance of their nation, but for themselves anticipating no changes but the few vicissitudes of their calling, they expect to live, till they lie down to sleep with their fathers, as calmly, as unknowing, and as unknown as they. But what a change passes over their lives from the moment they connect themselves with Christ! They become witnesses of the most wonderful events, and are in a school that will make them the most wonderful men of all recorded time. Soon a power is conferred upon them, and a work is intrusted to them, which cast into utter insignificance the authority and pomp of kings. "Home, kindred, country, they forsake. Their nets may hang and bleach in the sun; their boats may rot piecemeal on the shore; for the owners of them are far away, sailing over seas to which that of Genesareth is a pond; exciting whole cities and countries to wonder and tumult; answering before kings; imprisoned, persecuted, tortured"; but everywhere gloriously carrying on a work as God's instruments, which will hand down their names to all ages, and in time change the face of the whole world. Instruments of God, indeed, they must have been, for how soon would a work so begun, and carried on by such men, have come to naught, if it had not been of God.

We have said that these men were in a school. Such, indeed, was the influence of the great Teacher to which they were now subjected. Under him they acquired new principles of action. Gradually did the characters of all the disciples experience a great change. They were made to feel that there was a bondage, worse than that of Rome, from which they were to be delivered; that there was a more blessed kingdom than one of outward glory and power, which Christ came to set up; and that into this they could be received only by most intimate acquaintance, in heart and life, with deep spiritual truth. How great a change, then, in the views and characters of these men, was wrought by their personal intercourse with the Saviour! Observe that it was brought about, not by any sudden and supernatural wrench of their natures, but by the natural processes of enlightening the mind, purifying the affections, and reforming the life. And what a testimony to his power, and to the power of his religion, was it, that these humble and untutored fishermen of Galilee had their hearts filled with a sublime and world-embracing purpose, and were armed with a spirit by which they went forth to a greater work than man had ever before conceived, and by which they triumphed and were glorified.

But of all the disciples there was no one upon whom the influences of the Saviour's spirit and life seem to have produced so great an effect as upon John. During the early part of his connection with Christ, this disciple is occasionally presented to us in a light which does not win our love. The youngest, as before said, of the twelve, with little experience of life, and having strong feelings easily aroused, no doubt the title Boanerges, — son of thunder, — which Jesus early bestowed upon John (see Mark iii. 17), was suggested by his warm and impetuous temper. This same temper led him, when indignant at the conduct of the Samaritans, who refused to receive his Master into their city, to ask if fire from heaven should not descend and destroy them. Luke ix. 54. So, also, on another occasion, we have a manifestation of a spirit which we cannot commend. Eager for the establishment of the new kingdom, then supposed to be one of temporal power and greatness, it appears that John, with his brother James, made a request to Christ, either personally, as we infer from the account in Mark x. 35, or through their mother, as it would appear from Matthew xx. 20, that they might be first, and sit one on his right hand and the other on his left. It seems at first view difficult to believe that it could have been John, the gentle and affectionate disciple whom Jesus loved, that manifested such a temper as this. And yet have we not often found that persons, who possess naturally strong and easily excited feelings, become the loveliest characters we have ever known, if only those feelings are governed and balanced by a deep experience and discipline of religious truth?

In the latter part of his connection with Christ, John's character appears very different from what it appeared at first. We find no more instances of his hasty temper. That was subdued and governed by the mild rebukes and faithful teachings of his Master. Henceforth he became, what we everywhere find him to be, gentle, meek, full of reverence, confiding in his Saviour with a trust that never once wavered, and penetrated in his whole being with the spirit of love. How often have we known those who have natures made up of the richest elements, but who are exposed, through some one weak point, to shipwreck and ruin! When we see such cases, how much do we feel that man has need of a power to guide, guard, and preserve, to bind the conflicting elements within him into one well-developed and well-fortified character! We may still find that power, where John found it, in communion with Christ.

As we follow the history of this disciple, it is easy for us to mark the progress of the strong affection that grew up between him and his Master and Lord. Thus John was selected by Jesus to be, with Peter and James, a witness of some of the most important and trying scenes of his life, such as the transfiguration and the agony of the garden. So, also, at the ever memorable scene of the last supper, the position which John occupied at the table is a proof of the love which Jesus felt for him. He was leaning on his bosom ; that is, as it was the custom to recline at meals, and John was next to Jesus, his head was brought near his Master's breast; and this was a position which was reserved by him who gave an entertainment for the person whom he most esteemed. It was while this disciple was thus leaning, that Peter beckoned to him that he should ask Jesus who it was that should betray him. John did as he was requested, and Jesus indicated who the traitor was by giving Judas a sop. All this seems to have been done in private, and apart from the knowledge of the other disciples, and proves the great measure of condescension and confidence which was exercised by the Master towards this his favorite follower. John, then, had reason to style himself "the disciple whom Jesus loved" (xx. 2). All the members of that little band were dear to Jesus,—dearer than his own life. But for this one—young, confiding, reflecting his own gentle and affectionate spirit, with him in his trials and leaning upon his bosom—he felt a peculiar love. Who can say that our religion does not encourage particular friendship between kindred hearts, when we have this beautiful example in its very Founder before our eyes ? And as this friendship was declared before all, and was acknowledged by all, and allusions to it therefore could give no offence, how gratefully sensible of its value does John prove himself to have been, by assuming no other name in his history than the disciple whom Jesus loved! What other words could add any thing to these ?

The next notice we have of John is at the crucifixion. He was the only one of all the twelve who had the fortitude to go to that scene of suffering and danger. Says the writer before quoted, in his life of this Apostle,—"How touchingly is it manifested on this awful occasion, that the softest natures are often the noblest and the most fearless too, and that those which are apparently the most daring and masculine may yet shrink away in the time of peril and distress! Who in that hour of darkness,—darkness in the heavens and in the hearts of men,—who in that hour of abandonment, when even the Son of God cried out that he was forsaken,—who of all his followers were with him then, to support him by their sympathy, and prove to him their love? In the midst of scoffing soldiers and brutal executioners, under the lowering sky, and just below the frightful cross, we behold four weeping *females* and *one* disciple, the youngest and the gentlest of the twelve, braving the horrors of this place of blood, braving the anger of those in authority and the insults of those who do their bidding, determined to be near their Master in his agonies, and ready on the spot and at the moment to share them. And what is it that braces up the nerves of this feeble company to such a singular pitch of fortitude and daring? The simple but unconquerable strength of affection; the generous omnipotence of their attachment and gratitude. In the might of their love they ascend the hill of Calvary, and take their station beneath the cross, hearing nothing amidst all that tumult but the promptings of their devoted hearts, seeing nothing but their dying Lord, remembering nothing but that he was dear to them, and that he was in misery. O, how loftily does courage like this rise above that ruder and earthly courage which rushes to the battle-field, and is crowned with the applauses of the world! It calls for none of those excitements and stimulants from without, which goad rough spirits into madness, but relies on those resources that are within, those precious stores and holy powers which are the strength of a single and faithful breast. That is the courage of the animal; this is of the soul. It is pure; it is divine. It was such as moved the complacent regard of the Saviour himself, even in the height of his sufferings. Hanging on the cross bleeding and exhausted, yet when he saw his mother and the disciple whom he loved standing by, he was touched by their constancy; his thoughts were recalled to earth; the domestic affections rushed into his bosom; and with a tender care, which provided at once a protection for his parent and a reward for his friend, 'he saith unto his mother, Woman, behold thy son! Then saith he to the disciple, Behold thy mother!' Where was there ever so affecting a bequest as was then made, when love and filial piety triumphed over suffering? Where was there ever so affecting an adoption as that which then took place, when attachment and fidelity triumphed over fear? The last earthly care of Jesus was accomplished. His mother was confided to the disciple whom he best loved. The favorite disciple eagerly accepted the honorable and precious charge, for 'from that hour,' as we are told by himself, he 'took her unto his own home.'" John xix. 27.

We next meet with John at the resurrection of Christ. Informed by Mary Magdalene, who went early to the sepulchre, that the stone had been rolled away, both John and Peter ran eagerly to the spot, and found the tomb empty. And here a slight circumstance is mentioned, which shows that John was more quick than all the other disciples to understand the words of Christ. They knew not the meaning of the saying that Christ must rise again from the dead. So unprepared were they for his resurrection, that Peter, when he saw the body was not there, did not ascribe the fact to its true cause. But John saw and believed. John xxviii. 8.

"It was into the mind of the beloved disciple that the light first broke. He first believed the glorious truth, that death was vanquished by the Son of God, and that Jesus of Nazareth was the Prince of Life."

Not long after this, when Jesus appeared to his disciples for the last time before his ascension, he foretold Peter's violent death; and that disciple, seeing John just behind him, desired to know what his lot was to be. The answer of Jesus was, "If I will that he tarry till I come, what is that to thee?" This answer caused a saying to go abroad that John should not die. We shall soon see what was the probable meaning of these prophetic words.

When finally the Saviour left the earth, and in obedience to his words the disciples came together at Jerusalem, John was there with them. His name is the third in the list given by Luke in the beginning of the book of Acts. But little is said of the part which John took in the missionary labors of the Apostles. We are only told, that once he was imprisoned with Peter, and once went with that disciple to teach in Samaria. It is at this point that the Scripture account of John closes. All early testimonies agree that he continued to reside in Judea, constantly taking filial care of Mary till the time of her death, which occurred about fifteen years after the ascension of Christ. John does not appear to have become a preacher to the Gentiles until after the destruction of Jerusalem. This event occurred in the year 70, and when John was about seventy years of age. It was this event, as is generally understood, to which Jesus referred, when he intimated that John should tarry until his coming, — his second coming in judgment upon the Jews. John was the only one of the first disciples who lived to see the holy city overthrown, her glorious temple destroyed, and the very ground on which it stood ploughed up by the hands of the Gentiles. Prior to this event, Matthew had published his Gospel in Judea, and had suffered martyrdom in Ethiopia; Mark had published his Gospel at Rome, and had died in Alexandria in Egypt; the aged Luke had published his Gospel in Greece, and had there gone down to his grave; and all the rest of the twelve, Peter, James, Andrew, Philip, Thomas, and Bartholomew, though meeting for the most part the death of martyrs, had yet finished their course with joy. John still survived to bear the testimony of an eyewitness of Jesus to a generation that succeeded these holy men.

What remains to be said of him may be very briefly told. He journeyed to Ephesus, in Asia Minor, and presided over the church in that place. In the persecution of the Christians under the Emperor Domitian, about the year 90, John was banished to the isle of Patmos. Here, as is commonly supposed, he wrote the book of Revelation. Under the successor of Domitian, John was permitted to return to Ephesus, where he soon published his Epistles, certainly the first Epistle, about which there has never been any dispute, though the genuineness of the other two has been sometimes called in question. Soon after this John wrote out his Gospel. We have been distinctly informed what was his object in doing this. It was to correct some errors prevalent at Ephesus, and to supply what was omitted in the three other Gospel histories, each of which he had seen. After this, John lived to attain the age of nearly one hundred years. His image is presented to us as a man bowed down with age, the sole living eyewitness of events the most memorable which the world has ever known, his whole heart and life imbued with the gentle, heavenly wisdom which he had learned from the lips of his Divine Friend, and devoting his failing strength to teaching that peculiar spirit of the Gospel on which he so much delighted to dwell, — its spirit of holy love. The following story of his last days is well authenticated, and is fully recommended by its perfect conformity with his character. It is said, that, when the infirmities of age so grew upon him at Ephesus that he was no longer able to preach to his converts, he used to be led to the church at every public meeting, that he might say to them only these few words, "Little children, love one another." And when they, wearied with the constant repetition of the same thing, asked him why he persisted in saying this, his reply was, "Because it is the command of our Lord; and if we do nothing more, this alone is sufficient."

He peacefully closed his long life, just at the beginning of the second century after Christ.

Such was the life of that disciple whom Jesus loved. Let us not fail to mark what encouragement to the humblest Christian there is in the fact, that the character which Jesus loved was such a character as this. It was made up, not of those shining, brilliant qualities which are possessed only by the few, but of that gentleness, meekness, reverence, faith, love, which we all may acquire, and by which we, too, may commend ourselves to the love of our Divine Master and Friend. So, also, in the fact that it was such a disciple as John that Jesus most loved, we may find new confirmation of the pure and holy purpose of Christ's mission. Had Jesus been bent upon accomplishing some great outward change for his own glory and fame, it seems inconceivable that he should have attached himself to the gentle, humble, retiring spirit of John. Had the fishermen of Galilee contrived the whole Gospel history, we know that a far different spirit than this of John was the popular Jewish spirit of those times; and how surely would they have represented some one like the bold and ambitious Peter as the favorite disciple! Or, in whatever age or land we suppose the Gospels to have been forged, let us ask ourselves, where or when has such a man as John been one of the world's honored ones? The spirit which made him the beloved disciple could have been no other than that which looks beneath all outward distinctions to what is in man's heart and soul, which, far more than the noisy gifts that the world has always honored, prizes humility, gentleness, and love, and which recognizes in manifestations of these the character that is truly good and great. Such we know was the spirit of Christ. The greatness which he loves, and to which he directs our aim, is the greatness that belongs to the highest part of our nature, which we share with children of God, with angels and spirits of the just made perfect.

CHAPTER XIII.

THE GOSPEL OF JOHN.

As respects the immediate motive which induced John to write his Gospel, we have the words of two independent authorities, which, as they come from an age soon succeeding the publication of this Gospel, and from the most distinguished writers of those early times, have ever been regarded as throwing a trustworthy and highly important light upon this subject. One of these writers has these words: — "John, desiring to extirpate the errors sown in the minds of men by Cerinthus and his followers, published his Gospel." — *Irenæus.*

This statement, that John had some reference in his Gospel to a peculiar and pernicious philosophy that prevailed in his time at Ephesus, is confirmed by several other sources. What this philosophy was, we shall have occasion to see hereafter. The other writer to whom we referred has these words: — "The first three Gospels being now delivered unto all men, and to John himself, he approved of them, and confirmed the truth of their narrative by his own testimony." — *Eusebius.*

We find this statement fully substantiated by an examina tion of John's Gospel. It bears frequent marks that he had seen the three preceding histories. Matthew, Mark, and Luke, as we all know, have the same facts in common. It was John's object, on the other hand, to pass by all that they had related, and to glean up what they had omitted. Accordingly, in his whole Gospel, with the exception of the events attending the crucifixion, there are but three facts which he has in common with the other Evangelists. Two of these — the feeding of the five thousand (John vi. 5), and the voyage connected therewith (John vi. 17) — he has repeated, because they were indispensable as introductory to the discourses that follow. The other is the account of Mary's anointing Jesus (John xii. 3), which John has recorded fully for a reason to which we shall soon refer. The beginning of miracles in Cana of Galilee, the raising of Lazarus, the conversation with the woman of Samaria, the washing of the disciples' feet, and the discourses and prayers uttered by Jesus just before his crucifixion, — these are instances of his supplying what the other writers had omitted, all these being found in John's Gospel alone.

This Gospel presents still another remarkable appearance, which confirms the historical account, that its author had seen the three preceding narratives. He frequently alludes to facts recorded in those narratives, without giving any relation of them himself. Thus he presupposes his readers to have knowledge of them by means of the other Gospels, and without this knowledge his own history would be in many places unintelligible. A few illustrations of this remark may be here named.

Before giving an account of the question that arose between the disciples of John the Baptist and some of the Jews about purifying, our Evangelist says, "John was not yet cast into prison." John iii. 24. And yet in the whole of this Gospel there is nothing said about John's imprisonment. The Evangelist presupposes his readers acquainted with that fact from the other Gospels, in which it is distinctly related. Nor is this all. Why should this fact of John the Baptist be here inserted at all? Evidently it is not required as an explanation of the narrative in this Gospel, for this nowhere implies that the Baptist was now or at any time imprisoned. It has the appearance, therefore, of a correction of other accounts, which had fallen into a slight inaccuracy. Such a correction is really applicable to two of our Gospels. Matthew says, directly after the temptation, before Jesus is related to have gone to Capernaum, that John had been cast into prison. Matt. iv. 12. Mark retained the same statement. Mark i. 14. The Gospel of John represents that the discussion about purifying took place after our Lord had left Capernaum, and had made a visit to Jerusalem, and was on his return to Galilee. John iii. 24 was intended to correct the inaccuracy of Matthew and Mark, who had antedated the imprisonment of the Baptist.

When Jesus washed the disciples' feet, we read (John xiii. 4), that he took a towel and girded himself, and poured water into a basin, *the supper being ended*, as the words read with which this beautiful incident in the life of Christ begins. The supper here referred to was undoubtedly the last supper, that supper at which John was present; for he leaned upon his Master's bosom, and saw all that was done, and heard all that was said. Yet this Evangelist has given no account whatever of that event. He found it correctly described by the other Evangelists, with whose accounts he presupposes his readers to be familiar, and hence his mere allusion to it would be at once understood.

In like manner, also, John remotely alludes to Christ's baptism (John i. 32), although the history of that event is totally omitted by him. Indeed, we should not be able to understand to what the language of this passage referred, did we not possess from another quarter the information which is here presupposed.

Thus there is a clear and marked agreement between the historical account, that John had seen the other narratives before writing his own, and the appearances of his Gospel itself. He evidently passes by what they related, supplies what they had omitted, alludes to facts attested by them as familiarly known, while in some cases he evidently retouches their narrative in order to correct some slight inaccuracies into which they had fallen. Beside the instances already given of such a revisal, two others may be here briefly alluded to. One is the account of the anointing of Jesus. John xii. 3. This is one of the few facts which John has in common with the other Evangelists. They have related it imperfectly. Matthew and Mark state that the woman anointed the head of Jesus; Luke, that she anointed his feet, and that she wiped them with the hair of her head. The former state the dissatisfaction of Judas respecting it, while Luke mentions the reproach of the Pharisee, and the rebuke he received. Add to all, that these Evangelists do not agree in assigning the same period for the occurrence of this event. For this reason, John goes carefully over the whole history of the incident. He combines in one clear narrative the broken and fragmentary accounts given by his predecessors, while he fixes the time of this anointing to be just before the betrayal of Christ, by showing that it was one of the causes which hurried on that event, since Judas, failing of getting money, as he had hoped, by the sale of the ointment, goes directly and bargains, for thirty pieces of silver, to give his Master up. The history of the resurrection is another example of John's revisal of the narrative of the other Evangelists. Matthew's account of this event is hurried, and both Mark and Luke have neglected to indicate the exact order in which the occurrences succeeded one another. John departs from his usual rule of not repeating what the other Evangelists had already recorded, and re-writes their account,—tells the whole story over again. John xx. 1. When we compare his narrative with that of his predecessors, we shall see that the former is the most intelligible and complete.

These facts are minute in themselves, and yet how important that they should be known! What evidence do they give of John's great care that an exact narrative should be handed down! What stronger confidence may we place in the narratives of Matthew, Mark, and Luke, when we know, that, though written at different times, in different countries, by different men, and for different classes of readers, they yet needed such few, and for the most part unessential, corrections! And what an interesting fact is it, that in the good providence of God all these different histories, before they were committed to the ever-flowing stream of time, were seen by one of the first disciples and constant eyewitnesses of all that they relate, and were by him carefully examined! Nor is the manner in which he corrected their mistakes and supplied their deficiencies less worthy of our grateful notice. John did not destroy the writings of his predecessors, and give us a history that rests on his name alone. He drew up his own more accurate and independent account, to be placed *by the side* of their histories, so that we might see both their text and his commentary, their errors and his corrections. Thus his Gospel sheds light upon their meaning, and gives new strength to their authority.

John's Gospel has a peculiar interest and value from another source. His historical scene is different from that of the other Evangelists. He records for the most part only what is done in Judea, just around Jerusalem, while the other writers record for the most part only what is done in Galilee, around Capernaum and the lake. When they conduct Jesus to the borders of Judea they there lose sight of him, and John takes up the narrative and accompanies him in his course. He, however, does not follow him back into Galilee, but forsakes him on the borders of that country, where the events of his life had already been related by Matthew, Mark, and Luke. How naturally does the explanation of this fact suggest itself to our minds! As the disciples were natives of Galilee, what Jesus said and did there would most interest them, and would be by them most clearly understood. When after their Saviour's crucifixion they became preachers in Jerusalem, it was of what transpired in Galilee that they would more frequently speak. Their hearers had heard of the events that occurred in their own city and neighbourhood. For this reason, they would ask about the scenes that were witnessed in the remote province of Galilee, where Jesus spent most of his time and performed the most of his miracles. We have seen that the Evangelists afterwards wrote their histories very much as they had orally told them, and hence it is easy to see why their historical scene was chiefly Galilee. It was John's care, therefore, in supplying the deficiencies of his predecessors, to describe what was said and done in *Judea*,—a task for which his long residence in Jerusalem of fifteen years, when he had the affectionate charge of Mary, the mother of Jesus, peculiarly fitted him. Without John's Gospel, the story of the Saviour's life would have been but little more than half told; but with this, the history is made full and complete.

In noticing some of the peculiarities of John's Gospel, we must not pass by its introduction (John i. 1–18), though it would be wandering from our purpose to dwell upon it long. Before we can understand this proem, we must know something of that peculiar philosophy to which we referred at the beginning of this chapter. This philosophy was called Gnosticism; Ephesus was its seat; and Cerinthus, one of its leading advocates, was expounding its doctrines in that city at the very time John was there writing his Gospel. It is not easy in a few words to describe this philosophy, because it is so foreign to our modes of thought. It may be sufficient to say, that the Gnostics referred all evil to matter, which they believed was created, not by God, but by an inferior divinity, called by them Demiurgos. The space between this inferior God and Jehovah was occupied, as they supposed, by various orders of angels, to which they applied the names *light*, *life*, and one of great distinction they named the *logos*, or *word*, whom they regarded as an impersonation of the power of God. All these angels emanated from God, as the light of one lamp emanates from another. They were employed in creating parts of the universe. They were not admitted into the presence of the Supreme, but inhabited a remote place in the heavens, called *fulness*. This philosophy was a subtile compound of Pagan, Jewish, and Christian doctrines, and throughout the early ages of the Church it threatened to be the most fatal foe to the simplicity that is in Christ.

Not improperly, therefore, does John, writing in Ephesus, begin his Gospel with an allusion to this heresy. Every sentence of this introduction is an affirmation against some Gnostic tenet. The logos or word was in the beginning, not created in time; with God, not inhabiting a part of the remote heavens; it was God himself, not a distinct angel; and it was the same in the beginning as now, not something that has undergone an emanation. It made all things. Life and light flow from it, and are not distinct angels. And then the Evangelist proceeds to show how a witness to the true light was raised up, and how at length the power of God became incarnate, and dwelt among us in the glory of the Only Begotten of the Father.

We have one mode of expression among us not wholly unlike those used by the Gnostics. We sometimes speak of *nature* as something distinct from God. We say nature causes the seasons to change, and the flowers to appear. If we annexed to our use of this word one or two other particulars corresponding to those ancient beliefs, such as these, that nature is an angelic emanation from God, and made only a part of the visible universe, and lived remote from the Supreme, we could confute such a system in no better words than these: — "In the beginning was nature, and nature was with God, and nature was God. All things were made by nature. And nature became incarnate, and dwelt among us the Only Begotten of the Father."

In this introduction we thus see nothing contradictory to what is so clearly and solemnly affirmed in the eighteenth verse of this chapter. Taken as a whole, instead of being obscure, it is of plain, weighty significance, and instead of being misplaced, it constitutes an appropriate introduction to the narrative that succeeds.

Thus far we have spoken of causes that give interest and

value to the Gospel of John, arising from the circumstances under which it was composed. It also possesses great interest and value from the peculiar character of its author. How does his gentle and loving spirit breathe from every part of it! It has been called "a tale of the affections," and it merits this title. In all his descriptions, John appears to set forth those scenes, and to dwell fondly upon them, which appeal to the deepest and tenderest emotions, — the marriage supper at Cana, the conversation with the woman of Samaria, the raising of Lazarus, the last interviews the Saviour had with his disciples. So, also, John was preëminent in his comprehension of the entirely spiritual nature of the new religion. He saw and felt that this religion was an inward life, a principle in the heart, calming all passions, calling forth the deepest treasures of love, trust, and joy, and making the soul one with Jesus and one with God. The other Evangelists have given us a plain, straightforward statement of facts. The whole Gospel history passed through their minds without receiving any coloring from themselves. It is well for us that it did so. We have before observed how much we owe to the fact, that these writers were simple, unlettered men, through whom the history of Christ comes down to us in the naked simplicity of bare facts, without any comment or coloring of their own. But when we have learned the facts from the other Gospels, what devout reader of the New Testament does not turn with refreshing interest to the warm, glowing writings of John? In these we see the action of Christian truth upon his heart. His remembrances of Christ's words and deeds clustered around the two great features of his own character, — love to God and love to man. And this spirit of love, presiding over every description and hallowing every scene, gives a subduing and quickening power to his narration. This is doubtless the reason why Christians in all ages have felt the greatest interest in the Gospel of John, have read it the most, and have dwelt with most fondness upon its words of tenderness and love. The early fathers of the Church used to say that the other Gospels were the letter, this was the spirit; the others were flesh, this was soul; the others were earthy, this was heavenly. But all such comparisons are unjust. They tend to exalt John's narrative by depressing the works of his fellow-laborers. They are all of heaven, and of the spirit that maketh alive. They are all in remarkable keeping with the character of the men that wrote them. They all have that variety, and were composed under those peculiar circumstances, which may justly give us the greatest confidence that they contain words of soberness and truth. We should thank God, then, for them all. They are his precious gift to us, providentially made in the beginning, and providentially handed down to us as the rich legacy of ages.

Of John's power of description, we may take his account of the raising of Lazarus as an example. John xi. 18–44. The story is told with few words, with plain words; yet all is so natural, so graphic, so full of life, that we seem to see the whole scene before us. It seems, at first view, unaccountable that this surprising event should have been omitted by the other Evangelists. It was one of the most astonishing acts of the Saviour's life; it was most publicly done, in the suburbs of the capital, in open day, in the presence of many witnesses. It is impossible it should have escaped the memory of any Christian historian of the time. Why, then, have Matthew, Mark, and Luke passed it by?

How naturally does a circumstance, mentioned incidentally by John, account for their profound silence! We read that after the miracle many of the chief priests determined to kill Lazarus, because his presence among the Jews had led many of them to believe in Jesus. John xii. 10, 11. Consequently, to publish this miracle while Lazarus and his sisters lived in Jerusalem was only to set up that worthy family as marks to the malice of the enemies of the Christian name. During their lifetime, therefore, the Evangelists, it is probable, refrained from descriptions of this event, and habits of narration may have led to its omission even in distant places, where, as in the case of Mark and Luke, the full record of it might have brought no harm. But the reason for omission here alluded to did not exist in the case of John. He survived Lazarus and his sisters, and when they had died and were beyond the reach of their foes, he gives a full history of the miracle.

As another instance of John's power of narration, look to the long interview Jesus had with his disciples just before the crucifixion, as described by this Evangelist, from the beginning of the thirteenth to the close of the seventeenth chapters of his Gospel. There is no part of the Gospel narrative more deeply affecting than this, and we shall do well to observe the order of events and the train of reflection, which will be now stated in the words of another.

"Judas, the betrayer, had left the company to commit his traitorous act. Now, said Jesus, is the Son of Man glorified. I am but a little while with you. I leave you the commandment of love which I have exemplified. He then exhorts his disciples not to despond at his death. He is going to his Father to prepare a place for them. He then utters his farewell; but says he will come again. Then he bids them rise and go hence.

"While they were seated, the discourse maintained the tender form of conversation. But after having risen he proceeds to exhort them to united and persevering efforts in concurrence with his purposes, and with increased earnestness he admonishes them to love each other and himself, and to expect, and to endure with a resigned temper, a cruel lot. Again he promises them the spirit, begins to mention more frequently his approaching death, and silence now reigns among the disciples. No one presumes to speak. Once only they question among themselves what is the meaning of the words, 'A little while and ye shall not see me, and again a little while and ye shall see me.' He perceives this, and explains himself. They believe that they now understand him.

"Then the occasion becomes more solemn. The discourse takes a higher tone. Jesus stands at the goal of his career. His conscience bears him witness that he has accomplished the mission given him by his Father, to bring truth into the world. With deep emotion he commends his disciples to his Father's protection, and not only they, but all who should believe in him. Every thought and feeling bears marks of belonging to that eventful hour.

"And is not all this in accordance with the character of Christ? Is it not the farewell of an exalted and noble soul, which, untroubled by the thought of impending suffering, occupies itself wholly with its lofty purposes, and with the business of instructing and consoling those whom it leaves behind? Could the gradation in the conversation possibly be more natural? Can there be imagined a more beautiful rise than is here presented, — first mutual remark, then increasing silence among the listeners, broken only by a low question, till ultimately the last whisper dies away, and in the universal stillness the soul mounts upward to its highest elevations?" *

---

* Hug's Introduction, p. 435.

Nothing but reality could have been the type of this. John wrote what he saw and what he heard, and on no other supposition can we possibly account for the wonderful record he has given us. And this same remark applies to all the Evangelists. That, in that rude age of the world, they should have conceived of a character like that of Christ, that all of them should have presented that one image, so sublime so godlike, without one thing to mar its perfect naturalness and consistency,—no, it could not have been, if there had existed no outward reality to give them the image they describe. And thus, how much easier is it to believe that the character made the biographers, than that the biographers made the character! Hence it was the confession of Rousseau, that " the fiction of such a character is a greater miracle than its reality." * Blessed be God that we have been taught to believe that it is a reality, that it was a living reality in the person of Jesus Christ, and may be now to a degree reproduced, a living reality, in ourselves! And to aid us in this great work, let us thank the Father of all mercies that we have these words written and sent down to us that we might have life.

---

* His precise words are,— " L'inventeur en seroit plus étonnant que le héros." —*Emile*, liv. iv.

CHAPTER XIV.

VIEW OF THE GOSPELS AS A WHOLE.

We have now looked at each of the Gospels as a separate and independent work. By combining the four narratives together, accepting whatever is peculiar to each, and dropping what is obviously mere repetition, we have one complete history of the ministry of Christ. Which Gospel comes the nearest to exact chronological arrangement, and for this reason should be selected as the basis of the rest? At first thought, it may seem as if this question must be answered in favor of Luke. His habits of exactness, and his declaration in the preface to his Gospel of his intention to write "in order" (Luke i. 3), appear to support such a claim. But the original word here translated "in order" has no necessary reference to the order of *time;* its meaning is as well expressed by the adverb *methodically;* while Luke's grouping parables together which we can hardly suppose to have been uttered at the same time, and his occasional indefinite allusions to times which are more carefully designated by Matthew, have led to the opinion that chronological order is not so generally marked by the former as by the latter Evangelist. In favor of Matthew it has likewise been urged, that, being a personal follower of Christ, he had means of knowing the exact chronology of events which neither Mark nor Luke possessed; and though Matthew shares this advantage with John, yet the purpose of this Apostle, as we have seen, was to supply what the other writers had omitted, and to make Judea chiefly the scene of his narrative. John's Gospel, therefore, so far from furnishing data for a chronology, needs a chronology elsewhere derived, to show the arrangement of its disconnected portions.

For these reasons, Matthew's Gospel has been preferred as the basis of a harmony. This point settled, every reader can easily make a harmony for himself. But little reference need be had to the Gospel of Mark. Only about twenty-four verses of this Gospel constitute additional matter; all the rest is found, either in the same words or in substance, in the other Gospels. Both Luke's Gospel and John's can be distributed without difficulty, each portion in its proper place, according to the chronology of Matthew. There is but one point which will occasion any perplexity. While the record of Matthew and Luke covers but two passovers in the ministry of Christ, John, on the other hand, appears to refer to three. It is believed, however, that this latter Evangelist does not in fact extend the ministry of Christ over a longer space of time than Matthew and Luke. The passover referred to in John vi. 4 is taken to be the same as that on which Christ was crucified. There is reason to think that John ante-dated the miracle of the feeding of the five thousand; and if we place the sixth chapter of his Gospel between those of the eleventh and twelfth, there is nothing to conflict with the chronology of Matthew. Many of the best authorities concur in this view of the case.

These hints are sufficient to enable any one to form a view of the life of Christ as a consistent and connected whole. Our present purpose is to speak of the moral impression which such a view leaves on the heart. This is one of the most convincing and satisfactory arguments for the truth of the whole Gospel history that can be offered. A plain, unlettered man is as good a judge of this argument, as is a scholar of the most extensive learning. Perhaps he is a better judge, inasmuch as he would be more likely to fall back upon the simple, natural feelings of his conscience and heart.

What, then, is the impression which a perusal of the Gos pel history naturally leaves upon the heart? It is that this is an honest book. Ten thousand unlettered and simple-minded persons read it, and they rise up with the impression that this is an honest book. They feel a regard for it, just as we all feel regard for a man in whom we discern marks of honesty, integrity, and truth, so clear and strong that we place the utmost confidence in him, and would trust him with any thing we possess. They believe it, just as sometimes in a court of justice a jury believes a witness who delivers his testimony with a simplicity, straight-forwardness, and sincerity which overwhelm all opposition, and carry conviction to the heart, even against much evidence on the other side. And they are right in placing reliance on these There is a heart knowledge as well as a head knowledge. We all feel that there is something in the higher manifestations of truth and uprightness which fraud and dishonesty can never put on. At any rate, the garments of truth do not sit easy and natural on the shoulders of a lie. A lie is something exaggerated and bloated; the dress it assumes will not stretch to cover it all up, and so the lie peeps out. But there is an ease and naturalness, an openness, an air of conscious integrity, which belong to truth alone. These are traits which strike the beholder at once. They speak to us with a voice of authority. We reverence them. We confide in them as we confide in nothing else. We find them our truest and safest guides.

It is not easy to analyze this impression which the Gospel history makes upon our hearts, and to say what all the elements are of our conviction that this is a true and honest account. Consider what your experience has been with some personal friend. You are satisfied he is an honest man. You feel that your property and character would be perfectly safe in his hands. But why you feel so, you might not be able readily to tell. Your conviction is the result of a thousand little circumstances which you would find it difficult to name, though hardly any more formal and tangible evidence could make it stronger than it is. So is it when we read the records of the life of Jesus. We feel that they are honest and true; but how shall we describe the causes which produce that impression, the delicate touches of reality and truth which we see on every page and in every verse, the sure tokens of uprightness and sincerity which the *heart* feels, but of which we give so poor account when we come to set them down in words?

Some of the reasons, however, why we *feel* that the Gospel history is honest and true may be named, and on the more obvious of these we shall now proceed to offer a few words.

The simplicity and artlessness of manner in which the Gospel history is told may first be named. Like honest witnesses in a court of justice, the Evangelists give their testimony with a plainness and straight-forwardness which find their way at once to the heart. There is no attempt whatever to set the story out, to dress it up, to round it off, to embellish it, no appearance of trying to make a show, of hunting after epithets, of straining for effect. Take any transaction they record, and an account of it cannot be given in fewer and plainer words than those which they use. They speak like men who speak from full hearts, who never once think how they shall speak, who only open their mouths and the fact speaks itself.

Again, what candid writers are these historians of the life

of Jesus! They appear to tell the whole truth, even when it makes against themselves and against the object they had in view in writing their histories, with just as much fulness and freedom as they tell any part of it. Thus, on several occasions, after our Lord had wrought some of his most surprising works, they say, "*Many doubted, some disbelieved, and would no longer walk with him.*" This is narrated without the slightest appearance of reluctance and hesitation. It cannot be said with propriety that the information is conveyed as a confession. It is given with the utmost freedom, with the air of men whose only concern it is to give all the facts in the case. They freely tell us, likewise, of their own prejudices, mistakes, gross ignorance, and faithlessness to their Master; and all this with no attempt to conceal their errors, with no affectation of humility, and with no parade of frankness. It all comes in as part of the history, in the same simple, unconscious manner in which the whole record is made.

Moreover, the narrative is not given by these men as if they felt that they had a case to make out. There is no attempt whatever to win the favor of their readers, no smoothing the story down so as to make it more acceptable, no fear lest you should draw wrong inferences, and not the least anxiety lest they should be disbelieved. Indeed, the bare possibility that they should be charged with falsehood seems never to have suggested itself to them. Their only concern is to tell the facts in the case. When they have done this, they leave them, with no preface, no argument, no comment, no exhortation, — without one single word asserting their veracity, or setting forth the importance and value of their history. They are witnesses and historians, and nothing else. Every thing is told with the air of impartial, almost of indifferent spectators.

We have before noticed the remarkable self-forgetfulness of these writers. Excepting a mention of their errors and mistakes, they never once, from beginning to end, allude to themselves. They say nothing of their feelings, of the wonder and awe, of the alternate hopes and fears, which must have possessed their hearts. You cannot find one single word which has the appearance of having been put in for the sake of bringing themselves forward. They are not brought forward. The reader of the Gospels does not feel that he is in the presence of Matthew, Mark, Luke, or John. He is in the presence of Jesus. He is a spectator of his wonderful works. He hears the words of one who spake as never man spake. And in this presence, the disciples felt every low, selfish, and personal motive subdued. When they came to write, they never once thought of themselves. "Filled with the grand truth of their subject, their own little feelings are all forgotten, or rather are totally subdued. The natural passions of human nature, which mingle with the thoughts of the wisest and best men, seem with them to have sunk down and become hushed in a hallowed calm."

In this life of Christ we discover no manifestations of any *party* feelings. These writers cherished a strong affection for their Master, but they never magnify him, never praise him; not one word of panegyric is there from beginning to end. There is not the least attempt to hold him up to our admiration; never once do they give expression to their feelings, when they saw him insulted, abused, smitten, and scourged. They give the bare facts in the case, and nothing more. So, on the other hand, they betray no desire to excite the passions of the reader against those who persecuted their Master. The Evangelists cherished no bitterness of feeling towards them. The very names of those who bargained with Judas, of the men who apprehended Jesus, of the officer who struck him, of those who afterwards did spit upon him, and buffet him, and mock him, and were loudest in crying "Away with him,"—of those, too, who upbraided him on the cross, and pierced his side with a spear, — the very *names* of those persons are not given. Even if these persons had been unknown to the disciples, angry and vindictive feelings would naturally have prompted them to seek out the names of those who made themselves so prominent in these cruel and disgraceful acts. It does not appear that the Evangelists did any thing of the kind. Here is a beautiful trait in their character. The reader is directed to a dissertation prefixed to Campbell's Four Gospels, where he will see it strikingly unfolded. This writer shows, that, of all the enemies of our Lord, the names only of the high-priest and his coadjutor, of the Roman procurator, of the tetrarch of Galilee, and of the treacherous disciple, are mentioned. In regard to the first four, the omission of their names could have made no difference, for the official title was equivalent in the case of such public men to a designation of the individual; while the part which Judas acted was too notorious to permit the suppression of his name, which, besides, would have cast a shade of suspicion over the memories of the eleven. But the names of those who befriended Jesus are carefully recorded, such as Simon the Cyrenian, who carried the cross, Joseph of Arimathea, Nicodemus, Jairus, Bartimeus, Zaccheus, Lazarus, Mary, and Martha. How strong the proof it furnishes, that these writers cherished no vindictive feelings, — that they did not write in the spirit of blind partisans!

The wonderful harmony in the portraiture of the character of Christ is the last circumstance which can here be named, as giving an air of truth and reality to these Gospel narratives. It is the same Christ in all; it is the same Christ in humble scenes and in great ones, at the marriage feast in Cana, and on the mount of transfiguration, by the well of the woman of Samaria, and at the grave of Lazarus, washing the feet of his disciples, and giving up his life on the cross. What a rare union of virtues seldom joined together, bending with grace to the lowliest act, and rising in majesty to the height of the sublimest! That four writers leagued together to propagate a lie should sustain throughout so peculiar and elevated a character as Christ's, should harmonize with each other in the delineation, and, not finding a type of truthfulness and purity in their own breasts, should draw a portrait so lofty, so spotless, so practical, so perfect, surely this was a prodigy which they could not achieve. "The fiction of such a character would be a greater miracle than its reality," and that the Evangelists had a living model before their eyes and hearts is the alternative of the most easy belief.

These are some of the elements of our conviction, that this history of the life of Christ is an honest book. The Gospels bear the impress of truth upon themselves. They are their own witnesses. They confirm themselves. The seal of honesty and reality is stamped upon them. The purest and the most elevated minds see it and welcome it; the very reading of this book lifts the mind up to its highest and noblest state, and the more we are enlightened and purified, the deeper is our conviction that here are words of infinite moment and worth. Nor are they men of learning and research alone who can share this conviction. Thousands of unlettered and simple-minded believers can have the same confidence and peace.

"A man of subtile reasoning asked
A peasant if he knew

Where was the *internal evidence*,
That proved his Bible true.

"The terms of disputative art
Had never reached his ear,
He laid his hand upon his heart,
And only answered, *Here*."

CHAPTER XV.

THE TRANSMISSION OF THE GOSPELS DOWN TO OUR TIMES.

How were the Gospels at first received and noticed? Into what hands from those of their authors did they pass? With what care were they treated? How were they kept? How extensively were they multiplied? Where were they deposited in that long night of darkness that has intervened between our times and the days of their authors? Where were they found, and how were they regarded, at the dawn of that light which awoke the nations from the slumber of ages? What circumstances attended their translation and compilation in the form in which we now receive them? These are questions of common importance to all Christians, and questions to which all ought to be able to reply.

Christianity was made known by the preaching of Jesus Christ and his Apostles. It was not at first introduced by a written document, like the ten commandments, which were graven on tables of stone. It was *preached*, in various countries, by men who had learned it from the mouth of its Founder. Hence their first duty was different from what it might have been had they lived in a country where printing and reading were as common as they are with us. Instead of writing the history of the life and words of Christ, we have seen that the Evangelists went everywhere preaching that history. When communities of believers were multiplied, and the Apostles had more demands than they could attend to personally, there arose the necessity of written documents, to go where they could not go, to answer inquiries, and to enlighten and confirm believers. The importance of securing these was still further apparent, by the approach of the time when all the first preachers of the Gospel would be removed by death. As soon as this event had taken place, and John, the last survivor of the disciples, had died, at the beginning of the second century, the writings of the Evangelists were held in the highest regard. These writings were appealed to as writings, as the received and authentic histories of Christ; they were cited by name; the names of their authors were given, and frequent quotations were made. These facts are important, as they show that our Gospels were in the hands of the immediate successors of the Apostles, while many were yet living who were contemporary with at least one of the original witnesses of our Saviour, and companions of his life.

The Christian writers who lived in the age next succeeding the Apostles are called the Apostolical Fathers. Quotations from their writings, amply confirming what we have here stated, may be found in all works on the evidences of the genuineness of the Gospels. A few may be here presented.

Papias was pastor of Hierapolis, A. D. 116. He was acquainted, as he says, with many of the disciples of the Apostles. In a treatise, entitled Explications of the Oracles of the Lord, he has these words: — "Matthew wrote the divine oracles in the Hebrew tongue, and every one interpreted them as he was able." Again he writes, — "Mark, being the interpreter of Peter, carefully wrote down all that he retained in memory of the actions or discourses of Christ."

Justin Martyr was a native of Samaria. In the year 150 he addressed a Defence of Christianity to the Emperor, Antoninus Pius; and in the year 162 made another defence, which was addressed to Marcus Antoninus. In these works he speaks of the memoirs which are called Gospels, and distinguishes between those written by the Apostles and those by the companions of the Apostles, that is, between Matthew and John, and Mark and Luke. He tells us how these sacred books were read in the assemblies of Christians on the Lord's day, and how reverently they were regarded.

Another of these early Christian writers, whose works have come down to us, is Irenæus. He was born, as is generally supposed, at Smyrna, about the year 150, received his Christian education from Polycarp, a disciple of St. John, was pastor of the church in Lyons, and, finally, suffered martyrdom, A. D. 202. Writing in the defence of the Christian faith, he says, — "We have not received the knowledge of the way of our salvation by any others than those through whom the Gospel has come down to us; which Gospel they first preached, and afterwards by the will of God transmitted to us in writing, that it might be the foundation and pillar of our faith. For after our Lord had risen from the dead, and the Apostles were clothed with the power of the Holy Spirit descending upon them from on high, were filled with all gifts and possessed perfect knowledge, they went forth to the ends of the earth, spreading the glad tidings of those blessings which God has conferred upon us, and announcing peace from heaven to men; having all, and every one alike, the Gospel of God. Matthew, then, among the Hebrews published a Gospel in their own language; while Peter and Paul were preaching the Gospel at Rome and founding a church there. And after their departure, Mark, the disciple and interpreter of Peter, himself delivered to us in writing what Peter had preached; and Luke, the companion of Paul, recorded the Gospel preached by him. Afterwards, John, the disciple of the Lord, who leaned upon his breast, likewise published a Gospel, while he dwelt at Ephesus in Asia. And all these have taught us that there is one God, the maker of heaven and earth, announced by the law and the prophets, and one Christ, the Son of God. And he who does not assent to them despises, indeed, those who knew the mind of the Lord, but he despises, also, Christ himself, the Lord, and he despises likewise the Father, and is self-condemned, resisting and opposing his own salvation; and this all heretics do."

Only a fragment of this father's writings have come down to us; yet so numerous are his quotations from the Gospels, that, when placed by themselves, they fill eleven closely printed folio columns.

Tertullian, the most ancient and most eloquent of the Latin fathers, was born in Carthage, where he was presbyter of the church, and where he became distinguished as a Christian writer about the close of the second century. No evidence from any writer, says Mr. Norton, can be more full and satisfactory than that which he affords of the general reception of the Gospels, and of their authority as the foundation of the Christian faith. There is not a chapter in the Gospels of Matthew, Luke, and John, from which he does not quote; and from most of them his quotations are numerous. Tertullian says, — "We lay it down, in the first place, that the Evangelic record had for its authors Apostles, to whom this office of promulgating the Gospel was assigned by our Lord himself. And if some of them were companions of Apostles, yet they did not stand alone, but were connected with and guided by Apostles. Among the Apostles, John and Matthew form the faith within us. Among the companions of the Apostles, Luke and Mark renovate it."

In Alexandria in Egypt, there was a celebrated school for the instruction of Christians, of which, near the close of the second century, Clement was the principal master. By him was preserved the same account of the formation and reception of the Gospels. "The Gospels containing the genealogies were written first. The following providence gave occasion to that of Mark. While Peter was publicly preaching the word at Rome, and through the power of the spirit making known the Gospel, his hearers, who were numerous, exhorted Mark, on the ground of his having accompanied him for a long time, and having his discourses in memory, to write down what he had spoken; and Mark, composing his Gospel, delivered it to those who made the request. Peter, knowing this, was earnest neither to forbid nor encourage it. In the last place, John, observing that the things obvious to the senses had been clearly set forth in these Gospels, being urged by his friends, and divinely moved by the spirit, composed a spiritual Gospel."

Origen was born in Alexandria, A. D. 185, travelled extensively in Palestine, Asia Minor, and Greece, became the most learned man of his age, and finally died about the year 253. He cites each of the four Gospels by name, speaks of them as "books in the most common use," "received without controversy," "believed in all the churches of God."

To these few examples, running back to the apostolic

age, and drawn from different countries, should be added the following important reflections by Mr. Norton. "In estimating the weight of this evidence, we must keep in mind, what has not always been sufficiently attended to, that it is not the testimony of certain individual writers alone. These writers speak for a whole community, every member of which had the strongest reasons for ascertaining the correctness of his faith respecting the authenticity, and, consequently, the genuineness, of the Gospels. We quote the Christian fathers, not chiefly to prove their individual belief, but in evidence of the belief of the community to which they belonged. It is not, therefore, the simple testimony of Irenæus, and Tertullian, and Clement, and Origen, which we bring forward; it is the testimony of thousands and tens of thousands of believers, many of whom were as well informed as they were on this particular subject, and as capable of making a right judgment. All these believers were equally ready with the writers who have been quoted, to affirm the authority and genuineness of the Gospels. The most distinguished Christians of the age, men held in high esteem by their contemporaries and successors, assert that the Gospels were received as genuine throughout the community of which they were members, and for which they were writing. That the assertion was made by such men, under such circumstances, is sufficient evidence of its truth. But the proof of the general reception of the Gospels does not rest upon their assertions only, though these cannot be doubted. It is necessarily implied in their statements and reasonings respecting their religion. It is impossible that they should have so abundantly quoted the Gospels, as conclusive authority for their own faith and that of their fellow-Christians, if these books had not been regarded by Christians as conclusive authority. We cannot infer more confidently from the sermons of Tillotson and Clarke the estimation in which the Gospels were held in their day, than we may infer from the writers before mentioned, that they were held in similar estimation during the period when they lived." *

Nor is it in the writings of Christians alone that we find testimonies to the reception of the Gospel histories, in the age that succeeded the Apostles. It was about the year 176 that Celsus wrote against Christianity. In his work, which has come down to us, he quotes the Gospels so frequently, as the admitted authority of Christians, that it has been said an abridgment of the history of Jesus might be made from his writings.

Thus there can be no doubt that our present Gospels were in common use at the close of the second century. "The number of manuscripts then in existence bore some proportion to the number of Christians, and this to the whole population of the Roman Empire." Gibbon estimated the population of the Empire, in the time of the Antonines, A. D. 180, at one hundred and twenty millions, and supposed that about "one twentieth part of the subjects had enlisted themselves under the banner of the cross." From these data, it has been estimated that there were at least three millions of Christians at the close of the second century. "There can be little doubt that copies of the Gospels were owned by a large portion of Christians who had the means of procuring them; and in supposing only one copy of these books for every fifty Christians, the estimate is probably much within the truth. This proportion, however, will give us sixty thousand copies of the Gospels" in existence at that time. See Norton, Vol. I. p. 52.

---

* Evidences of the Genuineness of the Gospels, Vol. I. pp. 150–152 (2d ed.).

As we come down to a succeeding age, we find that the progress of the Christian religion, and especially the fierce and wide-spread controversies that marked the third and fourth centuries, called for a rapid multiplication of copies of the Gospels. Translations of them were made into all languages that were then spoken, so that the life and words of Christ might be read, not only in Judea, but in Greece, in Rome, in Asia Minor, in Africa, in Egypt, in Arabia, in Gaul. Thus were produced Syriac, Grecian, Latin, Armenian, Ethiopic, Egyptian, Arabic, and Gothic translations. Nor was this the only effect of these controversies. They caused these Gospels to be most diligently studied; copies were compared with copies; the very words of the Evangelists were quoted as the ultimate authority to which all disputants must yield ; and so numerous and various are these quotations in the mass of the controversial writings which have come down to us from those times, that it is said, if every existing copy of the Gospels were now destroyed, the whole Evangelical narrative could be reproduced from the quotations found in the works of five writers alone. It is pleasant to see how the strifes of these ages, though in such terrible contrast with the mild spirit of the Prince of Peace, were yet made subservient, by Him who brings good out of evil, to an unspeakably important end. The fact should reconcile us to the divisions and controversies which still prevail in the Christian world. Who can doubt that these, too, are overruled for good?

That seemed an evil day for the Christian world when there sprung up so extensively a passion for building vast and massive convents and monasteries. In these, the piety and virtue of the times, instead of being like leaven in the corrupt mass of society, seemed to be immured and buried; and the active duties of a Christian life, which the world so much needed, were neglected for the visions and dreams of monkish cells. The unnatural and secluded life which men there led must have been unfriendly to the healthy piety even of the truly devout; while with others it favored the vices and crimes of which we have all read in history. Yet how great is our indebtedness to these establishments! They became the only safe depositories of the precious treasures of the past. Age after age these religious houses were quiet and undisturbed. Invading armies never attacked them; and while war demolished the fortresses and palaces of kings, the sword of the conqueror was never lifted against these shelters of peaceful piety dedicated to God. Within their walls alone were letters and science studiously cultivated, and thus they handed down the torch of learning from century to century. Every monastery had its library-room; not only a place of deposit for manuscripts, but a place where manuscripts were copied. Here, shut out from the strifes and cares of the world, many monks were always employed, year after year, in the quiet and patient work, so well suited to the lives they led and to the tastes they cherished, of multiplying copies of important writings; and by the vast number who were thus perpetually at work, copies were furnished with an abundance, and cheapness, and beauty, which even the art of printing has hardly rivalled. And then, when barbarous ages had passed away, and our modern civilization was established, and through the prevalence of the arts and blessings of peace a better day began to dawn, it was from these houses of religion that were brought forth all that we have of the records of ancient history, and poetry, and eloquence; and with them the manuscripts which bring down to us the life and words of Jesus. Vast numbers of them have been gathered from various lands, and in various tongues. Griesbach, a learned German scholar, consulted three hundred and fifty-five, in order to prepare his edition of the New Testament; and Michaelis carefully collated the greater number of four hundred and fifty. This is but a small part of all which are known to exist. Even to this day additional copies are found. A year or two since, forty were discovered in an old monastery in Upper Egypt, of various languages, some in the very dialect which was spoken by Jesus and his Apostles, and as old as the beginning of the fourth century. The owners of these manuscripts could not read the languages in which they were written, and probably these copies had been untouched for centuries, in the stone scriptorium where they were found. Had it not been for such arks of safety, thus provided, and guarded, and reverenced, we see not how these treasures of the past could have been so surely preserved to us. They were the fit instruments to accomplish the very work that was then needed. The perpetuity of the Christian religion seems to be owing in part to that cause which threatened its total corruption and death. What can be a more striking proof of God's making even the follies and superstitions of mankind subserve his own designs?

In 1360, a translation of the New Testament into English was made by Wickliff, "the morning star of the Reformation." He was born in Yorkshire, England, in 1324, and was rector of Lutterworth, in the diocese of Lincoln, till his death, in 1384. His manuscript was a translation from the Latin, and was circulated until it was suppressed by the Pope. Copies of it are quite numerous in the public libraries of England, and in the collections of private individuals.

The art of printing was invented in the early part of the sixteenth century; and the New Testament was among the books which first received the benefit of the invention. It was printed in 1514, at Alcala, in Spain, under the care of

Cardinal Ximenes, Archbishop of Toledo. Neither time, labor, nor expense was spared to make the work as perfect as the means would permit. Learned men were employed twelve years in comparing various manuscripts, and the expense of a small edition was fifty thousand ducats. "A singular fate attended the manuscripts from which this edition had been prepared. About fifty years ago, two German professors repaired to Alcala, to ascertain if they could be found. They learned, to their inexpressible disappointment, that, about thirty-five years before, the librarian, to whose care they had been intrusted, ignorant of their true value, sold them to a man engaged in preparing fireworks, and he had used them in making rockets."

In 1516, the second printed copy of the New Testament was published by the learned Erasmus, at Basil, in Switzerland. In 1546, a third printed copy was published at Paris, by Robert Stephens, who formed his edition by collating fifteen different manuscripts. In 1582, the fourth printed copy was published at Geneva, by Theodore Beza, who compared all the former editions with manuscripts which had not been consulted before.

The copy of the New Testament first printed in England was published in 1526, by William Tyndale. In 1535, it was again published in that country by Miles Coverdale. In 1611, the translation made by the authority of King James was published; and this is the version which is in general use to this day. The utmost care was taken by the king to secure an accurate translation. For this purpose he selected fifty-four of the best classical and Biblical scholars, in order, as he said, " that our intended translation may have the help and furtherance of all our principal learned men in this our kingdom." This number was reduced to forty-seven before they entered upon their labors. They were then divided into six companies, to which equal portions of the Bible were assigned. They held their sessions at Westminster, Cambridge, and Oxford, and were employed three years. Upon the completion of their work, a committee of six, chosen from the joint companies, began to review the whole. They met daily for nine months; and when at length the translation was published, it had such a character for accuracy, that, by general consent, all other translations have fallen into disuse.

At the present day, Biblical scholars find a few texts, in the received translation, which are of doubtful authority, some passages, also, which are obscurely expressed, and not unfrequently a word or phrase inconsistent with the present use of our language. These evils are slight, however, compared with the immense advantages of having the same translation used wherever the English language is spoken. Among these must be included, not only its effect in perpetuating the original character of the Anglo-Saxon tongue, but its moral effect, also, in preserving the unity of the Anglo-Saxon race.

Such has been the transmission down to us of the message which was brought from heaven by the mouth of the Son of God, and which was designed for the children of men in all after times. It would seem as if it was intrusted to very unsafe keeping, judging merely after the manner of men. It had no permanent memorials of brass or marble; it was in words only, and in words merely spoken, — cast forth upon the air. But those words were gathered up by faithful men, and though committed to frail materials of parchment, they have been handed down to us through ages which have crumbled marble to dust, and rusted all inscriptions from brass. Through what a long and revolutionary period of history have these words found their sure way! —

the controversies of the first centuries, the irruption of the barbarians, the dismemberment of the Roman Empire, the night of the Dark Ages, the revival of letters, the wars of the Reformation, the discovery and peopling of a new world. Indeed, the whole face of the earth has been changed,—all manners, customs, institutions, arts, and empire! Have the records of the Gospels been changed, or do we read the same words now which were read by the first Christian believers?

CHAPTER XVI.

THE EVIDENCE THAT THE GOSPELS HAVE BEEN TRANSMITTED WITHOUT CORRUPTION.

How do we know that, through all these countless changes, the Gospels have come down to us unchanged? May they not have been corrupted, by additions or perversions, so that we cannot now know whether they are worthy of implicit trust? The early rapid spread of Christianity is one security on this point. Before the Apostles died, churches had been established, not only in the principal places of Judea, but along the whole coast of Asia Minor, in Italy, and Greece; and before the generation that succeeded the Apostles had passed away, there were communities of believers in every part of the then known world. When these faithful preachers had gone to their reward, we have seen that their writings were at once the subject of a wide-spread interest. By every Christian they were regarded as of unspeakable importance. They were sought for and read, not only for the light and comfort of believers in their private devotions, but as a part of the regular service of the religious assembly on the Sabbath. We have before noticed the estimate which has been made, that, within a century after the Apostles, there probably existed fifty thousand copies of the Gospels, in different tongues, and in different parts of the world.

Now had Christianity possessed only a local interest, and been acknowledged only by a single neighbourhood of believers, who had but a few manuscripts of the Gospels, it would have been less difficult to corrupt these manuscripts, and deceive the community of Christians. But as it was, while we cannot suppose that the writings of the Apostles would be universally corrupted in the very age in which their authors themselves lived, so it seems utterly incredible that it *could* have been done in the age that succeeded. In our day, how impossible that a single false reading could creep, or be forced, into all Bibles, used in all families and churches, not in this nation only, but in all lands, and in all tongues! Human hands could just as easily introduce a new star into the firmament of heaven, or expunge one of those shining lights from the sky. Doubtless this impossibility is greater now than it was in the earlier days of Christianity; for such is the accumulative nature of this evidence, the uncorrupted preservation of the Scriptures has been rendered more safe by every step the world has taken from the time of their origin. More copies have been made, and they have circulated over wider portions of the globe. But the same kind of security against a corruption of our sacred writings has always existed, and it existed in the very age that succeeded the Apostles. In the thousand copies that were then made, translated into various languages, and sent into all parts of the then known world, we have a convincing proof that no accident or design could universally impair their purity and authority. It is true, that, by this multiplication of copies, the chances were increased for verbal errors to be committed. By the comparison of various manuscripts, many errors of this kind are found. A word is sometimes omitted, or misspelled, or transposed, a letter or part of a verse is left out. These various readings, as they are called, are counted by thousands. But not one in a thousand affects the sense, and not one in the whole number constitutes a turning-point of any doctrine or duty. Of so little consequence are the various readings occasioned by a multiplication of copies, while, in consequence of this multiplication, no *essential* errors could be introduced by design, or could creep in through mistake.

But who are the persons to be suspected of undertaking the work of corrupting the Gospels? "Human beings do not act without motive. If we suspect that our sacred writings were at an early period tampered with, either unauthorized additions made to them, or portions erased from them, we can probably give some reason for such an opinion. Who, then, are the persons that would undertake this work? Not Christians, certainly. They must have felt the strongest interest in preserving the purity of these writings. The religion they had embraced separated them from all other men, called them to a new life, gave them new sentiments, and hopes, and desires, demanded of them such a conscientious discharge of duty as had hardly before been conceived of, subjected them to privations and insults, to danger and death. That they should have been indifferent to the purity of those writings on which their faith rested, on which they had staked all their interests and all their hopes, is certainly most incredible." Not only would they not cause, but, as far as their watchfulness could go, they would not permit, the slightest change to be made in books whose sacredness and trustworthiness would be thereby impaired.

Shall we, then, say that corrupt changes of the sacred writings were made in the early ages by the enemies of the Gospel? But why should they set themselves to alter and corrupt what it was so much easier for them to destroy? Why resort to a process so tedious and difficult, and of extremely doubtful success, as that of attempting to weaken the authority and pervert the design of all existing copies of the Gospels by corrupting the text, while the far more obvious and practicable scheme for accomplishing their purpose was before them, — that of destroying the writings themselves? That this alone would appear the practicable course is not mere conjecture and opinion. It is proved to us by evidence and fact. In the persecutions to which the early Christians were exposed, we know that the destruction of their books was often attempted, and, so far as it could be done, it was carried into effect. They were time and time again burned, and all were forbidden to copy them under penalty of death. But we have no evidence and no hint, that the plan of destroying their value and use by corrupting the text was ever attempted, or even once thought of.

But it may be said, that in past ages all who have called themselves friends of the Scriptures have not agreed, any more than such persons agree now, in the interpretation of the Gospels; that we read that there were those in very early times who "wrested the Scripture" to favor their own views; and that, in the zeal of party strife, the sacred writings may have often been corrupted to support the opinions of particular sects.

We will not forget, however, that the very idea of a sect is a number of Christians cut off, or divided from, the body of believers; that the Scriptures have been in the hands of this body, as well as in the hands of the sect; and that if ever it has been for the interest of the minority to alter the reading of the Gospels, it has been equally for the interest of the majority to prevent such changes, and to preserve the purity and integrity of the text. The division of Christians into sects, then, so far from having endangered, has, in fact, secured the uncorrupted preservation of the Gospels. Some division has existed ever since some were of Paul and others were of Apollos. The Epistles furnish proof how many subjects of controversy agitated the first communities of believers. No one, who has read the history of the Church, will forget how early great and grave questions arose, which continued to divide the opinions of Christians down even to the establishment of the Romish Church. During the general sway of this church, there always existed independent communities that came not under its dominion, while many of the orders embraced in its folds were as much opposed to each other as have since been the Protestant sects. Thus, there has never been a time when an attempt to alter the text of the Gospels, even if otherwise practicable, would not have raised an outcry in some quarter or other. There has never been a time when Providence has trusted the legacy of the Scriptures even to their friends, without some safeguard for their protection and unadulterated transmission. One portion of believers has been a check upon another. In their mutual strifes, they have but one interest in common, — to exercise a jealous vigilance to keep the Scriptures in the same state in which they came into their hands. Any attempt, therefore, to alter them, for the purpose of favoring any particular scheme of doctrines, must have been, in the very nature of things, discovered and exposed.

We have before alluded to the great number of quotations from the Scriptures made by the early Christian writers. The first two hundred years after the death of the Apostles were most prolific of works of controversy, sermons, commentaries, annotations, and histories, — a whole body of literature, furnished by writers of different countries and of different tongues. Their writings have come down to us in manuscripts which are as authentic as any remains whatever of ancient letters. In these we find the words of the Gospels quoted just as we read them now in our Bibles, and so numerous are these quotations, that, as was before remarked, if the New Testament should at any time be annihilated, we could recover the book from the writings of that age. Here, then, is a most important and valuable test of the purity in which the Gospels have been preserved. Had those early authors cited many texts from the New Testament which we do not now find in our copies, we should know that parts of this book, in the course of its transmission to us, have been lost or suppressed. On the other hand, had they quoted other passages in different words, and as conveying different meanings from what we now find in our copies, we should know that such texts have been corrupted, either through accident or fraud. But as the quotations they make agree substantially with the text that we possess, and include almost every passage that we possess, how satisfactory the proof that the Gospels have suffered no essential changes, as they have passed from one generation to another, and are now what they were at first! This evidence is open to no uncertainty, and admits of no refutation. If we will not say that all remains of sacred and profane literature, of the first centuries of the Christian era, were the forgeries of some subsequent age, we must admit that these quotations bridge over the whole period of the Middle Ages, and carry us up to the generations immediately succeeding the Apostles, and show them reading the same Gospels which are now in our hands.

It is a still further important consideration, that the Gospels bear no marks of an age later than that in which it is affirmed that they were written. If they had suffered mutilations and additions from the hands of successive copyists, these alterations, it is likely, would be detected. Especially if they were numerous, if they were thrust in by ignorant transcribers, having different views and feelings, and more or less interested and excited about the opinions and controversies of their own times, how surely would these alterations have been discovered by something not consistent with the character of the sacred writer, by an expression of opinions and feelings which it is not probable that he entertained, by the use of language and the introduction of modes of conception not known at the period to which they are assigned, by an implied reference to opinions and events of a later age, or by some bearing and purpose not consistent with the time when they are alleged to have been written! These are but a few of the ways by which the work of those who had tampered with our sacred writings would surely have been detected. But no traces like these of corrupt changes of the text can be discerned. Says Mr. Norton, in the valuable treatise before referred to, and to which this chapter is so largely indebted,—"No one has yet appeared who has found any thing here which does not correspond to the age in which their authors lived, and to the circumstances in which we must believe them to have been placed."

So, also, had our Gospel histories suffered mutilations from many successive hands, their unity both of design and style would have been lost. Each writer has a way that is peculiar to himself; his style, mode of narration, choice of expressions, and form of presenting a subject, are all peculiar to himself. So strikingly is this the case, that it has been said, if a chapter from one book should be transferred to another book, having a different author, the transposition would, by the dissimilitude of the style, be at once detected by a critic. How irreconcilable with all this is the notion that these books have been brought to their present state by additions and alterations of successive copyists! Instead of the one distinctive character which each work has, a diversity of hands would have produced a diversity of style; and the patchwork of unknown and successive transcribers would have been a perfect contrast to the simple, uniform, unbroken narrative of the sacred penman.

The same general conclusion is fortified by one more consideration. It is impossible that the records of our faith should have been much corrupted, for whenever and wherever they have been read, men have gathered from them substantially the same Christian religion. Is there a single copy of the Scriptures, in any language, in any land, from which the honest inquirer would draw a different system of faith and practice, or a different representation of the Divine government, from that which he finds in the copy before him? Is there a copy from which a single article of our faith is absent? He who would weaken our confidence in the sacred writings, by suspicions of their corruption, should bring forward these conflicting and imperfect versions if he can find them. But this cannot be done. Wherever in the past ages we find men believing in the Christian religion, we find that they believed in the same religion that we believe in; they held to the same rule of life, referred to the same prophecies, related the same miracles, ascribed the same character to Christ, and were rejoicing in the same immortal hopes. How idle, then, to speak of corruptions which the text of Scripture may have suffered, when we see that it has thus spoken one and the same language to all! It is true, the mere letter has passed through many hands of copyists and printers, and has been rendered into many different tongues. But ever has it quickened the same spirit;

the piety that it kindled a thousand years ago is the same piety that it kindles now, and thus has the essential Gospel been, like Jesus himself, the same yesterday, to-day, and for ever.

How can we think of these things without reflecting with gratitude upon the course which Divine Providence adopted, to hand down the Gospel truth from one generation to another? Those frail records of the Evangelists were in fact the most secure means for the preservation of the life and words of Christ which could be employed. "A temple, a statue, a monument, is but one, and however durable may be the material, it continually decays, and is always destructible. The touch of the sculptor moulders from the chiselled surface, and the time will come when every monument of his genius shall have crumbled to the earth. The Pyramids themselves have grown old with age, have forgotten the names of their builders, and have long since betrayed their trust."

But written records are less liable to extinction than any other memorial of the past that can be devised. The sacred words, inscribed of old on parchment, soon found their way to every land, and the time has never been when they could perish or suffer corruption, except by a devastation that visited at once the whole face of the earth.

Thus has the past ever been safe. Thus, too, is the future ever secure. Amid all the revolutions and vicissitudes of earth, the Gospel will still be accomplishing the thing wherefor it was sent, and no one can turn it aside from its silent and steadfast way. The assaults of its enemies are in vain. The gates of death shall not prevail against it. The mouldering fingers of time, that efface every thing else, shall not destroy this. The grass withereth, the flower fadeth, but the word of the Lord abideth for ever.

www.ingramcontent.com/pod-product-compliance
Lightning Source LLC
LaVergne TN
LVHW021424110826
845150LV00007B/2068

* 9 7 8 1 4 2 5 5 0 8 5 1 7 *